Meaning in Law

Meaning in Law

A Theory of Speech

Charles W. Collier

OXFORD
UNIVERSITY PRESS

OXFORD
UNIVERSITY PRESS

Oxford University Press, Inc., publishes works that further Oxford University's objective of excellence in research, scholarship, and education.

Oxford New York
Auckland Cape Town Dar es Salaam Hong Kong Karachi Kuala Lumpur Madrid Melbourne Mexico City Nairobi New Delhi Shanghai Taipei Toronto

With offices in
Argentina Austria Brazil Chile Czech Republic France Greece Guatemala Hungary Italy Japan Poland Portugal Singapore South Korea Switzerland Thailand Turkey Ukraine Vietnam

Published by Oxford University Press, Inc.
198 Madison Avenue, New York, New York 10016

Library of Congress Cataloging-in-Publication Data
Collier, Charles W., 1950-
Meaning in law : a theory of speech/Charles W. Collier.
p. cm.
Includes bibliographical references and index.
ISBN 978-0-19-538897-8 ((hardback) : alk. paper)
1. Freedom of expression. 2. Semantics (Law)
3. Law—Philosophy. I. Title.
K3253.C65 2009
342.08'5—dc22 2009012969

---

1 2 3 4 5 6 7 8 9

Printed in the United States of America on acid-free paper

Contents

Preface

The announcement for the latest edition of a leading text on freedom of expression states that it "proceeds from the assumption that the variety of First Amendment values can best be studied . . . as they emerge from concrete cases rather than from an abstract characterization and classification." I think not. Nothing intelligible is likely to "emerge," unannounced, from the study of concrete legal cases.

Lawyers (and law professors) spend a lot of time debating whether, for example, a given law is "content-based" or "content-neutral" and whether legislative action is (or is not) "related to the suppression of free expression." I understand the need for these more or less inconclusive arguments. They respond to preestablished categories in legal doctrine, which in turn pose questions that need to be answered one way or another for a case to be decided. Good lawyers are adept at formulating arguments on both sides of these questions (which is why I call their arguments "more or less inconclusive").

Consider, for example, a city's ban on nude scenes in drive-in movies that could be seen from a highway. The city argued that its ordinance (1) protected people from movies that might offend them, (2) protected children from nudity, and (3) ensured that passing motorists would not be distracted. The debate then turned on (1) whether passersby could simply "avert their eyes"; (2) whether minors need to be protected from all nudity, "irrespective of context or pervasiveness"; and (3) whether soap operas or violence would be any less distracting to passing motorists. To which the Supreme Court added helpfully: "Such cases demand delicate balancing."

I think little is to be gained by pursuing this form of argumentation, and indeed the opportunity to approach the subject of speech from a more fundamental perspective is likely to be lost. Thus, I propose to disregard the "fundamentals" of legal doctrine (at least for a while) and to approach the subject with as few legal preconceptions as possible.

But I will not be sailing trackless seas. Arguments drawn from those disciplines one would most naturally consult in the study of speech (linguistic theory and the philosophy of language) will serve as important points of reference throughout. And when I do turn to concrete legal cases, my focus on "symbolic speech" will keep the definitional question ("What is speech?") at the forefront.

There is a certain schizophrenia involved in writing about speech from the perspective of linguistic theory or the philosophy of language, because "speech" is not the term (or the concept) that would be used in those disciplines. Instead, it is the term chosen by the framers of the Constitution's First Amendment, when they declared that "Congress shall make no law . . . abridging the freedom of speech." They did not choose to protect "language" or "expression" or "communication" or "symbolism," even though these are typically the uses to which speech is put. In a sense, "speech" in the legal context is whatever courts say it is; but I do not think that is a very important sense. In fact, it is very important *not* to think this way, because then all the natural, logical associations that might inform a general theory of speech are hostage to the peculiarities of legal doctrine. So while I shall pursue those natural, logical associations as far as possible, the tension inherent in the philosophical analysis of an irreducibly legal concept cannot ultimately be resolved.

Introduction

What do flag burning, cross burning, draft-card burning, nude dancing, wearing black armbands, and sleeping in public parks have in common? For one thing, they have all been considered "speech," for purposes of the First Amendment, by the U.S. Supreme Court.

Of course, none of the above activities is speech in any normal sense. They are what constitutional lawyers term "symbolic speech." More than two centuries of adjudication have extended recognition and protection to symbolic expression in a bewildering array of circumstances the Founding Fathers clearly never envisioned. Recent decades have seen a veritable explosion in types of protected symbolic speech but without a theoretical framework for such a development. It is nothing short of remarkable that, amidst this proliferation of contradictory and confusing legal decision making, neither courts nor commentators have seen fit to develop a general legal theory of "speech," language, or expression. This book addresses these issues and provides such a theory.

A FEEBLE PHILOSOPHY

Legal opinions rarely provide much of a theoretical framework for the decisions they justify, and in this respect constitutional, First Amendment decisions are no different from those in other areas of law. There are two main reasons why law's attempts at philosophizing must necessarily remain feeble at best.

First, legal decisions are made in the context of individual cases and on the basis of specific facts. *Ex facto jus oritur* (law arises out of facts). If the Hippocratic oath in medicine means "do no harm" to the patient, the analogous injunction in law is "do justice in the individual case." Another traditional legal maxim warns that "hard cases make bad law"—certainly a curious state of affairs from the viewpoint of systematic philosophy. If legal opinions were supposed to develop general theoretical frameworks, then hard cases would provide illustrative limiting examples marking the boundaries of legal doctrine. Instead, they seem rather to muddy and obscure those boundaries.

The second reason law cannot be philosophy relates to its structure of authority. Both the doctrine of precedent and the structure of appellate review ensure that lower-court judges trying to "do justice in the individual case" will proceed on the basis of higher courts' "institutional authority" and not on their own intellectual authority. Theoretical correctness and rational consistency have never been the coin of the realm in law. As Justice Jackson once remarked of the U.S. Supreme Court, "We are not final because we are infallible, but we are infallible only because we are final." Such a situation would never be tolerated in philosophy, where one is free to correct thinkers from Plato to Wittgenstein if their arguments are deficient.

Law is not philosophy; it is not supposed to be. There might possibly be some advantages in being governed by "a bevy of Platonic guardians," but we have not chosen to find out. Nonetheless, in First Amendment law at least, an underlying theory of decision making seems called for by the fact that so much turns on what counts as "speech." If there is to be a definition, then there should be a theory; and "speech," in its common acceptation, has always been too broad and universal a concept to be reduced to a mere legal term of art. Indeed, rather than restrict protected speech within narrow parameters, the clear judicial tendency has been to expand the notion broadly into areas of "symbolic speech" that would hardly have occurred to the framers of the Constitution.

So, how should one take account of these developments? Two main avenues suggest themselves. First is the method of *reconstruction,* that is, the attempt to derive a coherent, underlying theory of speech from the scattered, unsystematic pronouncements of individual jurists and legal commentators. Second is the method of *construction,* by which a theoretical framework for the legal doctrine of speech would be articulated anew on first principles developed in nonlegal disciplines. Each approach will be considered in turn.

RECONSTRUCTION

The implied theory of speech that can be reconstructed from scattered judicial opinions and legal commentary is necessarily only rudimentary and limited. Nevertheless, it provides a starting point. The basic problem is this: All speech (not just symbolic speech) involves some form of conduct as well. If the definition of speech were not further restricted or limited, courts would face claims that "an apparently limitless variety of conduct can be labeled 'speech' whenever the person engaging in the conduct intends thereby to express an idea."

To head off such claims—which could involve all forms of criminal behavior—courts have insisted on the following three limiting principles.

First, "conduct may be 'sufficiently imbued with elements of communication to fall within the scope of the First and Fourteenth Amendments.'" The requirement of "communication"—however ill defined—may be regarded as basic. And communication entails at the very least a speaker and an audience. In an early case involving students' refusal to salute the American flag, the Supreme Court noted that "[s]ymbolism is a primitive but effective way of communicating ideas. The use of an emblem or flag to symbolize some system, idea, institution, or personality, is a short cut from mind to mind." In that case, the Court concluded (in effect) that *not* saluting the flag was a form of speech. Likewise, in a case involving the state motto "Live Free or Die" on automobile license plates, the Court extended First Amendment protection to someone who (in violation of state law) merely covered up that motto. Although these decisions seem intuitively correct, surely more of a theory is needed to explain how *not* doing or expressing something can be "speech."

Second, for communication to count as speech, there must be "[a]n intent to convey a particularized message." This requirement was first enunciated and deemed satisfied in a case involving a peace symbol taped to an American flag. Nevertheless, in the leading flag-burning case, dissenting Justices argued that "[f]ar from being a case of 'one picture being worth a thousand words,' flag burning is the equivalent of an inarticulate grunt or roar that . . . is most likely to be indulged in not to express any particular idea, but to antagonize others." The contours of this requirement thus remain essentially contested.

Third, for the communication of a message to receive First Amendment protection, "the likelihood [must be] great that the message would be understood by those who viewed it." In the case of the peace symbol taped to the flag, the Court explained that "the context in which a symbol is used for purposes of expression is important, for the context may give meaning to the symbol." That case arose at a time of great national antiwar protests, so "it would have been difficult for the great majority of citizens to miss the drift of appellant's point at the time that he made it." On the other hand, in the case of sleeping in public parks, dissenters in the lower court denied that "sleeping is or can ever be speech for First Amendment purposes"—presumably no matter what the context. And in any event, courts have not explained why the audience should get to determine what counts as speech.

So much for the main principles implied in the legal discussion of symbolic speech. Such speech must amount to communication (in a sense yet to be defined), the speaker must intend to convey a specific message, and the audience must be able to understand it. These rudiments of a doctrine of speech seem reasonable enough as far as they go; but obviously they do not go very far. And it is not even clear why these particular principles should be the starting points for a definition of speech. To proceed beyond the stage of vague intuitions and everyday associations, it is necessary to go beyond the legal sources.

CONSTRUCTION

The method of construction addresses conceptual problems *de novo,* using the best and most appropriate analytical tools available, regardless of where they originate. Considering the limitations of the legal discussion of "speech" outlined above, why would anyone accept such limitations?

As noted already, the lack of a coherent legal theory has not prevented or even slowed down the proliferation of judicially recognized forms of symbolic speech. Indeed, the cases far outstrip the theory. In construing "speech" so broadly, the case law positively cries out for interdisciplinary support. Rather than depend on vague, intuitive, unrefined notions of *speech, communication, symbolism,* and *meaning,* it only makes sense to take advantage of long-standing discussions in other disciplines that systematically address these issues.

A proper theoretical treatment would also restore symbolic speech to its rightful place as the definitional key to First Amendment decision making. Ironically, it is the least central contexts of First Amendment law that provide the most important delineations of its coverage. Within a proper theoretical framework, illustrative limiting cases should serve to demarcate the outer boundaries of the legal doctrine of speech. But in the nude dancing case, for example, the Court was seemingly dismissive of this definitional value, noting only that "nude dancing of the kind sought to be performed here is expressive conduct within the outer perimeters of the First Amendment, though we view it as only marginally so."

The task of construction involves the use of relevant nonlegal disciplines, which in this case means seeking the conceptual basis of First Amendment law in linguistic theory and the philosophy of language. Chapter 1 begins with the philosophical theory of meaning and then shows how that theory needs to be broadened. Chapters 2 and 3 pursue the main conceptual stages in the expression of meaning: from symbols, through signs, to words. Chapter 4 pauses for a look back and a look forward, with special reference to the problem of drawing constitutional boundaries around "speech" in the case law of prior restraints, obscenity, and defamation. Chapter 5 returns to the analysis of symbolic speech in law, considered as a special case of the philosophical analysis of meaningful conduct. Finally, Chapter 6 applies the fruits of this analysis to the constitutional case law of symbolic speech.

★ ★ ★

Stylistic conventions: Words to which attention is being drawn and words used in an unusual sense or context are placed within quotation marks (sometimes known as "scare quotes"); words used as objects of linguistic study or as terms to be defined are *italicized.*

CHAPTER 1

Meanings

I.

Current philosophical discussions of meaning have been heavily influenced, informed, and inspired by ordinary linguistic usage. A number of important philosophical distinctions have been derived from various senses of the verb *to mean* and the different—even contradictory—ways it may be used. For example:

> [1] Those spots didn't mean anything to me, but to the doctor they meant measles.[1]

The spots cannot be viewed in any sense as "speaking," they have no intended audience, and there is no message that could be put in quotation marks (e.g., "You've got measles"); yet the word *mean* is used in a perfectly proper and ordinary way. I shall refer to this as *natural meaning*.

A different sense of *mean* is evidently at issue in the following example (which, incidentally, amounts to "symbolic speech" in the legal sense):

> [2] Those three rings on the bell (of the bus) mean that the bus is full.[2]

Here the bell ringer undoubtedly intends to send a specific message (probably something like "The bus is full") and is partly relying on the audience's recognition of his intention to do so. This is a case of *speaker's meaning*, which may be defined as what a speaker actually meant by uttering a sentence, "what a particular speaker intends to use a bit of language for."[3]

Finally, there are cases involving the meaning of sentences or expressions in the abstract—quite apart from their use by any particular speakers. For example:

> [3] The word "circle" means "a plane figure contained by one line such that all the straight lines falling upon it from one point among those lying within the figure are equal to one another."[4]

This is a case of *expression meaning* (or *sentence meaning* or *linguistic meaning*), which may be defined as what the expression really means in English, "the meaning an expression has in a language, independently of its use on particular occasions by particular speakers."[5] Expression meaning may not necessarily coincide with speaker's meaning, as the following example rather imaginatively illustrates:

> A man suddenly cried out "Gleeg gleeg gleeg!," intending thereby to produce a certain effect in an audience by means of the recognition of his intention. He wished to [report] that it was snowing in Tibet.[6]

This is supposed to be a case in which the conditions for speaker's meaning have been met, yet one might still wonder whether under the circumstances "Gleeg gleeg gleeg!"

meant anything at all (or whether the speaker was serious or even sane).[7]

Taking their point of departure from ordinary linguistic usage, analytic philosophers have been highly successful in making useful distinctions among these three fundamental senses of meaning.[8] Much important work has been accomplished along these lines.[9] And yet from another point of view, the really fundamental questions have barely been considered. What do these three divergent senses of meaning have in common? What is the same in all these cases? From the fact that something is meaningful, should we not proceed to ask what *makes* it meaningful?

In what follows, I shall systematically distinguish (1) "What makes *X* meaningful?" from (2) "What does *X* mean?" The first question seems more fundamental and seems to suggest a common element in the three different senses of meaning discussed above. Consider again the first example, the case of a natural pattern.

> Those spots didn't mean anything to me, but to the doctor they meant measles.[10]

By its own terms, this example sends a contradictory message. The spots "didn't mean anything" to the speaker of the sentence, who nonetheless consulted a doctor about them. Rational people do not consult doctors about truly "meaningless" spots. More likely, the speaker thought the spots meant *something*, without knowing exactly what. In other words, the spots were meaningful to the speaker, who nonetheless did not know what they meant. The spots were also meaningful to the doctor, who (unlike the speaker) did know what they meant. And we can imagine a third person to whom the spots truly "didn't mean anything" at all. This person sees no significant difference between spots and no spots; this person does not consult a doctor.

What made the spots meaningful to the original speaker? To answer this question, I propose a different hypothetical example taken from the field of paleontology. According to Charles Darwin, the fossil record is like "a book preserving just a few pages, of these pages few lines, of the lines few words, and of those words few letters."[11] Of course, Darwin mainly emphasizes how little of the rudimentary fossil "message" remains; but even here, he does not go far enough. Perhaps the most one can say is that under certain circumstances, the fossil remains can be meaningful to someone.

What might those circumstances be? Imagine a paleontologist at work in the field, sifting through endless pieces of shale. Mostly she encounters random variations in the rock, useless bits of meaningless detritus. "Of course it took hours and hours," reports one field worker, "but you saw everything yourself, and various things could sink in gradually."[12] What is the paleontologist looking for, waiting for? "It is so exciting to find those hidden things," writes the same field worker, and then more specifically: "It is an incomparable thrill to reveal *a hidden structure* in the rock."[13] The paleontologist looking for fossilized organisms is probably hoping to see an organized structure, an orderly form (like bilateral symmetry) emerge from the otherwise haphazard, chaotic mass of material.[14] To be on the safe side, let us say that the paleontologist is looking for something "different" or "special," and most of what she encounters is (by definition) neither.

Now imagine an astronomer seeking signs of intelligent life in other galaxies. "Astronomers interpret very weak signals that are buried in big noisy databases."[15] Let's suppose that for the express purpose of announcing their existence, intelligent beings in another galaxy have obligingly sent in our direction a collection of recognizable mathematical ratios (in the form, say, of music). (This would correspond to speaker's meaning.) Suppose further that our astronomer's radio telescopes are powerful enough to "eavesdrop" on yet another galaxy and to detect the radio signal of a musical score that is stored in electronic form in that galaxy's main library. (This would correspond to expression meaning.) For our astronomer, the two cases are indistinguishable; it matters not whether a musical message is intentionally being sent or whether he has inadvertently stumbled upon a composition in storage. In both cases, the distinctive mathematical ratios underlying the music will call attention to themselves against the "background noise" in his cluttered database.

Furthermore, the task of the astronomer (in either of the two scenarios) does not seem to differ materially from that of the paleontologist (with allowances for relevant differences in subject matter). They are both highly trained observers who can, under certain conditions, reliably identify something specific as meaningful against a generally irrelevant background. In other words (and despite surface differences in linguistic usage), natural meaning, speaker's meaning, and expression meaning all presuppose certain shared conditions for the possibility of meaningfulness.[16]

II.

Linguists and cognitive scientists have studied the roles of *prototypes* and *salience* in the specification of word meaning. A prototype may be defined as a leading example of a member of a class. Why, when asked to mention an animal, are people more likely to say "a dog" than "a fly" (even though they may have encountered more flies than dogs)? Why, when asked to mention a prime number, are experimental subjects quick to give the numbers three or five but not two or eleven? Why, when shown a picture of an oak tree and asked what it is, do subjects normally say "a tree" rather than something as specific as "a white oak" or as general as "a vegetable object"?[17] An answer may be attempted in terms of salience, but that only opens up a further line of inquiry:

> What makes for salience is hard to say. The honest answer is that we do not know. What we do know is that, up to a point, salience can be measured in terms of brain activity or psychological function. Thus, for individual occurrences to be salient they must raise the attention, which is a measurable parameter, and they will normally have a high rate of memory retention, likewise a measurable aspect. For features of objects to be salient they must satisfy conditions of prominence, and also be measurable. But this amounts to a recording of symptoms, not to a specification of what it is that makes for salience, and why. To answer those questions one needs an adequate theory of cognitive structures and processes, together with an appropriate theoretical language. . . . [18]

The following discussion briefly addresses these needs.

Consider this experimental situation. A subject sits in an auditorium in complete darkness. After some time has passed, a small point of light appears, projected on the upper front wall of the room. The point of light begins moving across the subject's field of vision. What would happen?

"It is known," reports the philosopher Maurice Merleau-Ponty, "that it is very difficult to fixate an object in a landscape illuminated by daylight for very long and, on the other hand, that a luminous spot in the dark exercises something like a power of attraction on the eye which it is difficult to overcome."[19] What is the nature of this "power"? Is it the power to *cause* the subject to look at the point of light and follow it with her eyes? In any event, that is what almost always happens. It happens with the kind of law-like certainty and regularity that in most other areas of life is fully sufficient to establish an empirical causal connection.

Yet, would we really want to say that the subject was in any sense *forced* to focus on the point of light, that she "had no choice" but to follow it? These are the sorts of things we are normally authorized to say when an empirical causal connection has in fact been established. Here, the subject might concede—at most—that the point of light was the most "interesting" thing in the otherwise dark auditorium; but nothing compelled the subject to look at it. This is not like a case in which physical contact causes an involuntary reflex reaction; nor is it like a case of being startled by a loud noise from behind or of squinting in sudden bright light. The subject is, in principle, perfectly free to concentrate on the completely dark 99.9 percent of the auditorium and simply ignore the tiny, remote point of light.

Yet, this is just what does not happen. Merleau-Ponty reports further that

> If, in the dark, a luminous spot appears in a marginal zone, everything takes place as if the equilibrium of the sensory-motor system were broken up; from this results a state of tension resolved by the fixation movement which brings the luminous spot to the functional center of the retina. Thus the motor devices appear as the means of re-establishing an equilibrium, the conditions of which are given in the sensory sector of the nervous system. . . .[20]

This "equilibrium" appears to be one in which the most interesting and important foci of attention are at the center of the visual field, where they can best be viewed. If they are not there already, the subject's focusing upon them will effectively "move" them to the center of the visual field, where they (in some sense) belong. In other words, the conceptual contrast between the important and the insignificant is translated into the perceptual contrast between the central and the peripheral.[21]

Gestalt psychologists have elaborated this "figure-ground" contrast as a basic structure of perception and behavior. But it is no less a basic—even *the* basic—structure of meaning.[22] Certainly it was at issue in the previous section, where the paleontologist and astronomer were looking for something "different" or "special."

By definition, everything cannot be different or special; the terms themselves are inherently contrastive.[23] It does not require much of a leap to say that the paleontologist and astronomer dismissed most of the "background" material they encountered as a precondition of finding something truly meaningful; it likewise seems safe to assume that for the subject in the darkened auditorium, this darkness—as compared to the point of light—is the perceptual equivalent of meaninglessness.

But it is not the darkness, as such, or any properties of the light, as such, that accounts for their meaningful combination. This is shown in Merleau-Ponty's observation that "it is very difficult to fixate an object in a landscape illuminated by daylight for very long," but that it is easy to do so in darkness.[24] Assuming that the light on the object is the same in both background situations, the varying *contrast* is what makes the difference, not any inherent properties of the light as such.[25]

The contrastive structure of meaning is also evident in the nature of memory. We might think of our memories as akin to data in a computer waiting to be retrieved, snapshots in a photo album waiting to be reviewed, or a film waiting to be replayed. The basic idea is that "everything" would be represented in memory, in the same proportions and relations as had originally prevailed; the contents of memory would objectively mirror the past. But current research on memory suggests a very different model:

> [W]e do not record our experiences the way a camera records them. Our memories work differently. We extract key elements from our experiences and store them. We then recreate or reconstruct our experiences rather than retrieve copies of them. Sometimes, in the process of reconstructing we add on feelings, beliefs, or even knowledge we obtained after the experience.[26]

Indeed, contemporary researchers explicitly invoke the contrastive terminology of "figure-ground" to explain the normal functioning of memory: "[P]eople usually remember well the central focus of an emotionally arousing incident, at the expense of poor memory for peripheral details. . . . [W]e remember more high and low moments from our lives than mundane ones."[27] The normal functioning of memory is thus driven more by categories of meaningfulness than by objective imprints of the past.[28]

> What we already know shapes what we select and encode; things that are meaningful to us spontaneously elicit the kind of elaborations that promote later recall. Our memory systems are built so that we are likely to remember what is most important to us.[29]

Consider for a moment what life would be like if this were not so.[30] Suppose that every time you tried to recall an episode from your life involving a table, all the memories you ever had involving tables were equally available to you. "There are probably hundreds or thousands of such incidents. What if they all sprung to mind within seconds of considering the cue? A system that operated in this manner would likely result in mass confusion produced by an incessant coming to mind of numerous competing traces."[31]

In *Funes, the Memorious,* Jorge Luis Borges describes a man who remembers *everything*. For Funes, "the present was almost intolerable it was so rich and bright; the same was true of the most ancient and most trivial memories."[32] Where we might, for example, see a wine glass on a table,

> Funes saw all the shoots, clusters, and grapes of the vine. He remembered the shapes of the clouds in the south at dawn on the 30th of April of 1882, and he could compare them in his recollection with the marbled grain in the design of a leather-bound book which he had seen only once, and with the lines in the spray which an oar raised in the Rio Negro on the eve of the battle of the Quebracho.[33]

Whereas we can recognize distinct geometrical shapes like the circle and rectangle, Funes recognized as distinct shapes "the tempestuous mane of a stallion, a herd of cattle in a pass, the ever-changing flame or the innumerable ash, the many faces of a dead man during the course of a protracted wake."[34] He even invented his own numbering system using a "rhapsody of unconnected terms"—more than twenty-four thousand in all—instead of numerals.

> Funes not only remembered every leaf on every tree of every wood, but even every one of the times he had perceived or imagined it. . . . It was not only difficult for him to understand that the generic term *dog* embraced so many unlike specimens of differing sizes and different forms; he was disturbed by the fact that a dog at three-fourteen (seen in profile) should have the same name as the dog at three-fifteen (seen from the front).[35]

Despite his general admiration for Funes, Borges "suspect[s], nevertheless, that he was not very capable of thought." To abstract—to generalize—is to ignore or, as Borges puts it, "to forget a difference."[36] Funes cannot forget.

To protect us from this potentially debilitating condition, the adaptive function of *forgetting* is also structured around categories of meaningfulness. "We are better off forgetting trivial experiences than clogging our minds with each and every ongoing event, just in case we might want to remember one of those incidents someday."[37] And yet, we also want to construct a reasonably accurate picture of the past out of our memories. These competing demands are reconciled as follows. In general, "information that is unimportant or no longer needed will tend not to be retrieved and rehearsed, thereby losing out on the strengthening effects of post-event retrieval and becoming gradually less accessible over time."[38] One researcher found that she was able to recall accurate details of specific events up to about one year later. "[B]ut beyond a year this event-specific knowledge began to lose individuating detail, and particular episodes began to merge into one another—they became general events. . . . [L]osses at the event-specific level can be turned into 'gains' at the general-event level."[39] Only if a specific event or detail was particularly consequential for us and our view of the world would—and should—it be able to resist this gradual process of absorption into general background knowledge.

III.

Relational meaning is a close cousin of contrastive meaning, of which it may be considered an extension or generalization. Contrastive meaning derives from the relations between figure and ground, the central and the peripheral, and the important and the irrelevant. Relational meaning broadens this notion to encompass more than one such contrast and potentially to include multiple levels and gradations of contrast.[40] Music, for example, is melody plus harmony plus rhythm.

Consider this experiment suggested by Victor Zuckerkandl in *The Sense of Music.* I play a Beethoven Bagatelle for you, but instead of playing through to the finish, I stop one measure short of the end. What is your reaction? It is probably something like that of Zuckerkandl's typical audience: "Why did you not finish? This is not the end. Something is missing here."[41]

Assuming you have not heard the piece before, how did you know that was not the end? Zuckerkandl says it is because "the tones must have some sort of meaning . . . in reference to which their sequence may appear complete or incomplete."[42] But how can a mere sequence of tones—especially ones you have never heard before—have that kind of meaning?

To answer this, let us work backward from the experience of incompleteness. Under the right conditions, a sequence of tones can create certain *psychological expectations* in the normal listener (who may or may not be able to say what the tones "mean"), and when those expectations are disappointed, the feeling of incompleteness results. Exercising his poetic license a bit, Zuckerkandl describes this "dynamic" quality of tones as "something we sense in the tone, a state of unrest, a tension, an urge, almost a will to move on, as if a force were acting on the tone and pulling it in a certain direction."[43]

These psychological expectations of the musical audience are, in turn, the product of skillful manipulations of certain key intervals between musical tones. No one tone can create such expectations. "[O]ur hearing of melody is not a hearing *of* tones but *between* tones—. . . music occurs not in the tones but between them."[44]

Clearly, the meaning of a musical melody is "relational" in the sense that it does not depend on any inherent properties of its constituent tones, e.g., pitch, loudness, duration, tone color (timbre), or volume. Each of these acoustical properties can easily be measured with an oscilloscope; but the relational qualities a tone assumes in a given melody do not register at all. In fact, none of the actual physical manifestations of a melody make it what it is. The melody can be played on a trumpet, clarinet, or xylophone. It can be whistled, hummed, or sung. It can be transposed up or down seven octaves or played in any key whatever. So long as the relations between the tones are preserved, the melody remains the same.[45]

It is easier to demonstrate the relational nature of musical melody than to explain precisely how its meaning arises. As noted above, one tone does not a melody make. But assuming a sequence of tones, what distinguishes a meaningful melody from the sound of a cat running across a keyboard? Zuckerkandl points to "some kind of pattern established by the piece itself,"[46] which is perhaps a good starting point. If it is to create the psychological expectations that define the dynamic quality of melody, the pattern must be strategically structured around certain key musical intervals such as the tonic, dominant, and subdominant.[47] Here one can speak only of probabilities, not certainties. In order to determine even something so basic as whether a piece is written in a major key or its relative minor (which has the same key signature), "we must hear or see a little of the music itself."[48] If a particular tone is returned to time and again as the resolution or conclusion of major phrases, one can provisionally term this the tonic or "key" of the piece—unless, of course, some sort of special effect is being set up to upset settled expectations. One is free to start off a melody in any direction whatever, but once a discernable pattern has been established, increasingly strong presumptions tend to rule out competing interpretations. "[O]nce it did take [that] step," says Zuckerkandl of a certain melody,

> nothing on earth could give that move another meaning than "in conformity with the acting force, reaching the center," and make us hear in it anything but a move from an unbalanced to a perfectly balanced state. Just as strictly and unequivocally will the meaning of any other move be determined by the prevailing dynamic situation.[49]

"Prevailing dynamic situation"—that is a good metaphor for the background conditions of relational meaning in any context. Musical melody is a relatively impoverished representational language, but precisely because it is "about" so little, it provides a particularly clear illustration of relational meaning in the abstract.

> [I]f we were to find a copy of a play by Shakespeare or a novel by Jane Austen from which the end was missing, we would at once be aware of the lack. But this is at least in part because words refer to objects and concepts of the "real" world—we know that the novel is incomplete because some event towards which the author has obviously been pointing does not occur. Musical tones, however, rarely convey any concrete meaning.[50]

Melody in the service of lyrics or a libretto occupies something of an intermediate position. To advance to the truly defining stages in the expression of meaning, we must turn to symbols, signs, and words.

CHAPTER 2

Symbols

As compared to musical melody, symbols are more strongly representational; it is much clearer what they are "about," and there is much more for them to be about. For example, a blindfolded woman holding a balance is a symbol of justice. Very few other things can provide such a fitting physical representation of the salient features of justice. There is a *reason* for this symbol. According to the most authoritative linguistic definition, symbols show "at least a vestige of natural connexion" with what they symbolize.[1]

I.

The standard account of symbolism starts not with symbols but with what they symbolize. If the world of symbols is in some sense an ideal world, then the real world is what they symbolize. The real world lies open to direct inspection and tangible sense-experience. The objects in the real world are as rich, full, concrete, variegated, and multifaceted as our senses can convey.

The real world provides the objective basis, the directly and immediately given point of departure, for all symbolic flights of fancy. It is the substratum to which they must ultimately return or refer and with which their truth or validity must be compared. Measured against the standard of objective reality, all symbolic representations must necessarily fall far short of that original. "For all mental processes fail to grasp reality itself, and in order to represent it, to hold it at all, they are driven to the use of symbols. But all symbolism harbors the curse of mediacy; it is bound to obscure what it seeks to reveal."[2] Symbols thus amount at best to pale imitations or faint copies of the immediate data of experience; at worst, they distort and misrepresent the true nature of things.

The real world is populated by objects of sense-experience. More specifically, we encounter "things," which always have "attributes." Our experience of these things always takes place in space and in time. The behavior of these things always fits within the scheme of universal causation and obeys all the known laws of nature. (When something violates these conditions, we call it a "miracle"; but no miracles have ever been reliably established.)[3]

This standard account is based on the commonsense theory of the world, or realism (sometimes termed "naïve realism"). Even so staunch a supporter of this theory as Karl Popper concedes that "[r]ealism . . . is not demonstrable; but while empirical scientific theories are refutable, realism is not even refutable. . . . [N]o describable event, and no conceivable experience, can be taken as an effective refutation of realism."[4] Popper relates the charming story of a certain Marie Ebner von Eschenbach who, as a young girl, would spin around suddenly to see if she could catch the world before it was able to reassemble itself out of nothingness. "[S]he was both disappointed and relieved whenever she failed."[5] But if Marie had succeeded, she would not have refuted realism; she would simply have discovered a surprising new fact about the world of experience.

Realism is not an empirical theory; our experience does not confirm it but rather presupposes it. No experience in the real world is imaginable without space, time, things, attributes, and causation. We might view it as an inherent limitation of the human condition that we can experience real objects only under these conditions. For us, these conditions define the class of "objects of possible experience." We might think of ourselves as simply unable to experience any other objects or to experience real objects any other way.

By definition, "objects of possible experience" are the only objects we can experience. In that sense, we ourselves set the minimum conditions for experiencing objects. (If something does not meet these conditions, then we cannot experience it.) One might therefore even say that we "impose" these conditions on all objects that we can possibly experience. This is in fact the position adopted by Kant, who compares it to Copernicus' famous shift in cosmological perspective:

> [E]ither I must assume that the *concepts* . . . conform to the object, or else I assume that the objects or, what is the same thing, that the *experience* in which alone, as given objects, they can be known, conform to the concepts. . . . For experience is itself a species of knowledge which involves understanding; and understanding has rules which I must presuppose as being in me prior to objects being given to me, and therefore as being *a priori*. They find expression in *a priori* concepts to which all objects of experience necessarily conform, and with which they must agree.[6]

In general, "we can know *a priori* of things only what we ourselves put into them."[7] Even in the natural sciences, the objects of physics do not coincide precisely with the objects of chemistry or the objects of biology, "because physical, chemical, biological knowledge *frame their questions* each from its own particular standpoint and, in accordance with this standpoint, subject the phenomena to a special interpretation and formation."[8]

The conditions for experiencing real objects are inherently relational in nature. To experience an object in time, it is necessary to think beyond the immediate "now" of the experience. The temporal now is experienced as the constantly moving boundary between the future (which it just was) and the past (which it is just about to become). Without these inherent references beyond itself, the now would become the timeless *nunc stans*, the very opposite of temporal succession. Time—as experienced—represents something else that is not—and cannot be—experienced (the future and the past).

It is likewise with space: In order for a single point to be experienced as somewhere "in" space, we must presuppose "a *system* comprising all designations of position. . . . In every element that we posit as spatial, our consciousness posits an infinite number of potential *directions*."[9] Similarly, our experience of a "thing" as more than the sum of its "attributes" is possible only if we have already adopted the perspective of the whole substance and distinguished that relatively constant whole from its variable parts. In this way, a variable quality "is not apprehended merely as a condition within me, but as a 'property' and objective quality, because I have already attained the desired function and perspective of the 'thing.'"[10] And finally, causation is the preeminent relational or contextual concept; "discursive" thinking views nothing in isolation but only as situated in ever-widening circles of etiological and teleological explanation. "Thus every separate event is ensnared, as it were, by invisible threads of thought, that bind it to the whole."[11]

These basic forms of mental synthesis and relation make experience as we know it possible and underlie all actual experience of objects in the real world.[12] In each of them, a present content of consciousness evokes other contents that are not immediately given; a whole is thereby represented or symbolized in and through each of its constituent parts. In this sense, our original experience of objects is already inherently "symbolic" or representational. Symbols cannot simply be faint copies of directly experienced objects; they are constitutive of that very experience itself. They make objective experience possible, and they make it what it is.

When we pass beyond the original experience of objects to that of artificially created symbols, we find the same function of representation at work. Only here, the pathways of representation are intentionally arranged—pre-arranged, as it were—for maximal evocative effect.

> Here consciousness, in order to apprehend the whole in the particular, no longer requires the stimulus of the particular itself, which must be given as such; here consciousness *creates* definite concrete sensory contents as an expression for definite complexes of meaning. And because these contents which consciousness creates are entirely in its power, it can, through them, freely "evoke" all those meanings at any time.[13]

If cognition, science, language, art, myth, and religion were measured by how well they *copied* objective reality, they would provide only very poor representations indeed. Instead, they create contrastive and relational meaning in their various media—sometimes more by what they leave out than by what they include. Artistic imagery (as opposed to mechanical reproduction) does not attempt to represent the totality of a given impression but rather selects certain "pregnant" factors; that is, "factors through which the given impression is amplified beyond itself and through which the artistic-constructive fantasy, the synthetic spatial imagination, is guided in a certain direction."[14] Into the symbol we compress—we concentrate—a totality of experience. As Ezra Pound abbreviated it, *dichten = condensare.*[15]

Paradoxically, we can attain a higher degree of objectivity with symbols than without them. The immediate contents of consciousness form a perpetually changing flow of phenomena that have, in themselves, "no rhyme or reason." Within this original flux, nothing ever remains the same or reappears in quite the same form. Pure immediate experience—without a contrast, without a context or bias or direction—would be completely meaningless, but our experience is not in fact so random or disoriented. "[W]ithin the sequence of these particulars we create definite intervals which provide a characteristic division and articulation" around "certain fixed points or resting places in this process . . . fixed centers of form and meaning."[16] Through symbolism, we are able to give form to an otherwise meaningless reality. A given particular content of experience is singled out and, without losing its character of particularity, is associated with a potential totality of such contents as their representative. We compress, as it were, a total phenomenon into one of its factors; we condense or concentrate it symbolically.[17] The particular thus represents a universal; it acquires in this way a definite ideal meaning that endures as such, beyond the transient phenomena of the individual consciousness.

Against the subjective play of passing appearances, the symbol then stands out as "the first stage and the first demonstration of objectivity, because through it the constant flux of the contents of consciousness is for the first time halted, because in it something enduring is determined and emphasized."[18]

II.

The farther back we trace the origins of symbols, the clearer their meaning becomes. It may not be an exaggeration to say that for primitive man, the whole world is symbolic. What we would consider actual historical persons, places, and events are all assimilated in primitive thought to timeless religious dramas and underlying mythical archetypes. Even today, in the "Holy Land" of the Middle East, otherwise barren, desolate patches of dusty desert land are thought to be "sacred" because something of religious significance supposedly happened there hundreds, even thousands, of years ago. Evidently, for the true believer, these are *more* than just patches of land; they point beyond themselves, they re-present something more important. But to the disinterested observer, the "sacred" land looks just like all the other land. Why should it matter if something important happened there many years ago?

"If we observe the general behavior of archaic man," writes Mircea Eliade,

> we are struck by the following fact: neither the objects of the external world nor human acts, properly speaking, have any autonomous intrinsic value. Objects or acts acquire a value, and in so doing become real, because they participate, after one fashion or another, in a reality that transcends them. . . . [E]verything which lacks an exemplary model is "meaningless," i.e., it lacks reality.[19]

For primitive man, the world itself is defined in terms of meaningfulness. It consists of the populated and cultivated regions, the navigable rivers, the charted seas, the mountains that have been climbed—in other words, "the world that surrounds us . . . the world in which the presence and the work of man are felt."[20] This world is meaningful because every aspect of it has a corresponding place in the parallel world of myth and religion, beginning with the myth of creation.

A certain plant might be highly valued not because it is precious in itself but because it refers back to the mythical, timeless past—perhaps it was first gathered by a god.[21] "[F]or the traditional societies, all the important acts of life were revealed *ab origine* by gods or heroes."[22] This means that "all the important acts of life" are symbolic in the sense that they merely represent and repeat episodes from a kind of master plan. In and of themselves and without supporting references to that master script, they have no meaning or value.

Beyond the boundaries of the meaningful world lie desert regions inhabited by monsters, uncultivated land, uncharted waters, and unclimbed mountains. These are all fittingly designated *terra incognita* on the ancient maps. In mythology they are assimilated to chaos, the formless void prior to creation. Here there are no rituals for erecting temples or blessing the first crops for the simple reason that there are no temples and no crops. Paraphrasing Wittgenstein, we might say that for primitive man, "the limits of my symbolism are the limits of my world."[23]

III.

One of the most fundamental symbolic functions is that of bestowing a name on something or someone. Naming is an angle from which to explore the notion of a "natural connection" between the symbol and what it symbolizes.

One of the oldest and most elaborate systems of naming is *totemism:* the primitive practice and institution of naming human social groups after animals, plants, and sometimes things. Once selected, the totem stands for and represents the tribe.

There is generally assumed to be some sort of natural connection—maybe even a necessary connection—between the human group and its totem. Summarizing this line of thinking, the social anthropologist Claude Lévi-Strauss observes that "[t]he beings which native thought endows with significance are seen as exhibiting *a certain affinity* with man."[24]

Is this "affinity" strong and deep enough to constitute a strict isomorphism, a one-to-one correspondence between some feature(s) of the human group and of the totem? The evidence seems to suggest not. It is known that totally different groups sometimes adopt the same totem, sometimes for completely different reasons. For the agricultural Indians of the American Southwest, the crow is regarded as a garden pest, whereas for the hunting and fishing Indians of the Pacific Northwest, it is a devourer of dead prey.[25] Likewise, various far-flung groups emphasize wholly different totemic aspects of the woodpecker: it inhabits the hollows of trees (Australia); its remains are never found (North American prairies); it is associated with tempests and storms (ancient Romans, Upper Missouri Pawnee); it is associated with the sun and stars (Osage); its song is "triumphal" and its alarm cry solemn (Iban of South Borneo).[26] When the same characteristic can be given different meanings—and different characteristics the same meaning—one cannot speak of a strict isomorphism.

Another theory posits an objectively perceived resemblance as the "natural connection" between men and their totems. But this would be difficult to maintain for the Azande, whose totems include such imaginary creatures as the crested water snake, rainbow snake, water leopard, and thunder beast.[27] Even among the Nuer, whose totems are at least real things,

> it has to be recognized that the list forms a rather bizarre assortment: lion, waterbuck, monitor lizard, crocodile, various snakes,

> tortoise, ostrich, cattle egret, durra-bird, various trees, papyrus, gourd, various fish, bee, red ant, river and stream, cattle with certain markings, monorchids, hide, rafter, rope, parts of beasts, and some diseases.[28]

Or consider how, among the Osage, eagles are interpreted as land animals: "[E]agles are associated with lightning, lightning with fire, fire with coal and coal with the earth. The eagle is thus one of the 'masters of coal,' that is, a land animal."[29] When anything can resemble anything else in this fashion, the notion of resemblance itself loses all meaning.

A final theory holds that the "natural connection" between man and totem is one of utility. Totems are selected because they are naturally most useful to man. A classic expression of this view is found in Malinowski's colorful description:

> The road from the wilderness to the savage's belly and consequently to his mind is very short, and for him the world is an indiscriminate background against which there stand out the useful, primarily the edible, species of animals and plants.[30]

But this "utilitarian" theory runs up against innumerable cases in which it is hard to see anything at all useful about the totem. To get around this difficulty, the notion of utility has been construed very broadly. Ursula McConnel interprets the totems of the Wikmunkan on the coast of Northern Australia as reflecting economic interests. This explains why the sea turtle, shark, crab, oyster, and other mollusks are totems. And it indirectly accounts for the thunder, "which announces the season of the north wind"; high tide, "which brings food"; and a little bird that is "believed to protect fishing operations." But even seemingly harmful things make their way onto the list because as McConnel explains, "totems may represent dangerous and disagreeable objects, such as 'crocodiles' and 'flies' which possess a negative social interest in that they cannot be ignored but may be increased for the discomfort of enemies and strangers."[31] As Lévi-Strauss observes, "it would be difficult to find anything which, in one way or another, positively or negatively (or even because of its lack of significance?), might not be said to offer an interest."[32]

These theories of a "natural connection" between man and his totems all fail for lack of falsifiability, which, as enunciated by Popper, requires at least enough empirical content for meaningful testing (and potential refutation).[33] There is no conceivable animal, plant, or thing that could not be explained and justified as a totem, either through the perverse but ingenious *bricolage* of the native or through the sophisticated semantics of the latter-day anthropologist. In the context of totemism, at least, the notion of a "natural connection" between the symbol and what it symbolizes is not based on empirical evidence in the scientific sense.

With respect to proper names of individuals, the situation is somewhat different. At least some of the personal names in traditional societies appear to have natural origins. In Llewellyn and Hoebel's *The Cheyenne Way*, for example, the following personal names appear: Red Robe, Two Twists, Pawnee, Wolf Lies Down, High Backed Wolf, Sticks Everything Under His Belt, Black Horse, Elk River, Cries Yia Eya, Chief Eagle, Walking Rabbit, High Forehead, Stump Horn, Calf Woman, Black Wolf, and Lone Wolf.[34] At least some of these names seem to reflect specific characteristics of their bearers; a man who goes by the name of "Lone Wolf" is probably not the gregarious "life of the party" (though one can only wonder what Sticks Everything Under His Belt was sticking under his belt). These names are descriptive, not arbitrary.

Even modern Western societies retain some vestiges of natural origins in personal names. Place of origin is indicated by French, German, and Dutch surnames beginning with *de*, *von*, and *van*, respectively. Names descriptive of occupations reflect their bearers' original occupations, if traced back far enough; at some point Mr. Baker actually was a baker.

But the clear trend is a transition away from common names to proper names, from descriptive to arbitrary names. John Stuart Mill captured this development correctly in observing:

> Proper names are not connotative: they denote the individuals who are called by them; but they do not indicate or imply any attributes as belonging to those individuals. When we name a child by the name Paul, or a dog by the name Cæsar, these names are simply marks used to enable those individuals to be made subjects of discourse. It may be said, indeed, that we must have had some reason for giving them those names rather than any others; and this is true; but the name, once given, is independent of the reason. . . . Proper names are attached to the objects themselves, and are not dependent on the continuance of any attribute of the object.[35]

Mill's observations are elaborated in a finding of cognitive psychology known as the Baker/baker paradox.[36] In this experiment, two groups of subjects are shown pictures of the same unfamiliar faces. One group of subjects is given the occupations of the people in the pictures; the other group is given their names. But: the occupations and names are designated by the same words. One group might be told that the first person was a "baker" and the second was a "potter." The other group would be told that the first person's name was "Baker" and the second person's was "Potter." The subjects are then tested as to how well they can remember each person's occupation or name.

The occupation names turn out to be significantly easier to remember than the proper names even though they are in all cases the same word. Why is it easier to remember a word treated as an occupation than that same word treated as a name? One reason may be that only the occupation names suggest "natural connections" with their bearers. They evoke a wealth of natural associations and are integrated in numerous ways with preexisting concepts and knowledge.

> [W]hen I tell you that my friend's name is John Baker, I tell you little or nothing about him, beyond that fact that he has a relatively common Anglo-Saxon name. When I tell you that my friend is a baker, however, I tell you quite a bit about him: a general sense of how and where he spends his days, what kinds of materials he uses at work, and what kinds of products he creates.[37]

You might know, for example, that bakers get up early, work in kitchens (around hot ovens), and bake bread and cakes.[38]

The proper name "Baker," however, serves as little more than a placeholder. Everyone has to have some name or other but beyond that, nothing ties Baker to the name "Baker," which might just as well be replaced with a number. The proper name thus functions more as an arbitrary designation than a descriptive title. Using the terminology introduced previously, the occupation name serves as a *symbol*; and anticipating terminology in the next chapter, the proper name serves as a *sign*.

The main development to be observed, with respect to names and to language generally, is the historical transition from symbols to signs, from natural connections to arbitrary designations. The symbolism of sacred places is perhaps most closely tied to nature, since the place itself typically "stands for" an earlier mythical or religious era in which that same, actual place figured prominently. But even then, the symbolic place is significant only as belonging to a "meaningful world" created by man, not nature. The institution of totemism brings with it a wealth of natural things to connect up with human groups, but it turns out that inherent natural affinities or preexisting natural connections explain almost nothing about which totems are actually selected. In the next chapter, it will be shown how the logic of totemic classification can much more plausibly be described as a system of relational meaning not unlike a language. Similar issues are raised by the transition from common names to proper names. For if the meaning of a name no longer depends on its connection to nature, that meaning can depend only on the place and role of the name in a larger relational system, created and institutionalized in human language.

CHAPTER 3

Signs

I.

The *sign* has a long and storied intellectual history, not all of which is relevant here.[1] One might begin by distinguishing natural from conventional signs and within the latter category, linguistic from nonlinguistic signs. Smoke, for example, is a natural sign of fire; a paw print in the dirt is a natural sign of an animal.[2] In both cases we reason from something that is perceptible to something that is not perceptible; in doing so, we reason back from an effect to what must have been its cause. (If something else could also have been the cause, then the effect is merely a *symptom*, not a sign.) This reasoning process is justified (only) if it is supported by reliable knowledge of the causal relations involved.

In the case of natural signs like the smoke and the paw print, we can normally assume that we have simply stumbled upon a bit of nature's causal processes at work; presumably, no one arranged the smoke and the paw print for us to find—no one is hoping we will make the correct inference from them to the fire and the animal. But now consider a conventional sign, like the three rings on the bell of the bus, discussed in Chapter 1. There, someone is very much hoping that we will make the correct inference from the perceptible sounds of the bell to their cause; indeed, it would be very strange and unusual for someone to ring the bell without hoping this (so much so that such a scenario can provisionally be ruled out).

In other words, the ringing of the bell is a sign of this hoping—this *intent*—that we infer from the ringing an imperceptible but intelligible meaning. We reason back from the effect to the cause, and here the cause is the decision to express an intent. "Conventional signs differ from natural signs," writes Pieter Seuren,

> in that the cause **C** of a natural sign is a natural cause, whereas the cause **C** of a conventional sign is the decision taken by a thinking individual to express . . . through a socially shared system of signs, an intent. . . . And since linguistic utterances are a subcategory of conventional signs, a linguistic utterance is a sign of . . . the presence of that intent.[3]

The bell ringer on the bus (as discussed in Chapter 1) intended to signal that the bus was full; more simply, therefore, the bell ringing meant "The bus is full."[4]

The above analysis may be summarized and at the same time extended as follows:

[i] The meaning of a conventional sign is its property of revealing an intent.

[ii] Intents are discursive; they involve complex thoughts that can be expressed intelligibly only in sentences, not individual words. A sentence (actual or implied) is the smallest linguistic unit in which an intent can be expressed.

Although it is convenient (and conventional) to think of the word as the prototype of the sign, it is difficult to assign any meaning to a word taken in isolation. To meet this difficulty, dictionaries typically employ two basic strategies: (1) defining a word in terms of other words (synonyms) and (2) displaying the use of a word in selected sentences.

The first strategy obviously involves a certain circularity. Take the word *Tier* ("animal") as defined in a leading German dictionary:

> A living being *(Lebewesen)* that feeds on organic material, moves, and reacts to stimuli.[5]

Lebewesen, in turn, is defined as:

> An organism *(Organismus)* with a living body and living cells.[6]

And *Organismus*, in turn, is defined as:

> An independent living being *(Lebewesen)* with a living human, animal *(tierisch)*, or vegetable body.[7]

We have now come full circle, it seems.[8]

The second strategy—displaying the actual use of words in sentences—has been employed with distinction by a number of leading dictionaries. "Having . . . no assistance but from general grammar," writes Samuel Johnson, "I applied myself to the perusal of our writers; and noting whatever might be of use to ascertain or illustrate any word or phrase, accumulated in time the materials of a dictionary."[9]

In his *New Dictionary of the English Language* (1837), Charles Richardson "almost entirely did away with definitions—but instead showed how each word had been used by illustrating usages with quotations. . . . He felt that only thus—by depicting a word's history, its *biography*—could the dictionary user have full and familiar knowledge of how best to employ the word himself."[10] Here is Richardson's own definition of *dictionary*, in its entirety:

> A book of words, containing (as distinguished from a mere vocabulary) their etymology, meaning, and usage.[11]

(There then follow eleven lines of quotations illustrating usage.)

This developing strategy was perfected, of course, by the *Oxford English Dictionary*, which enlisted "[a]n entire army" of volunteer readers who would "join hand in hand till it covered the breadth of the island . . . drawing as with a sweep-net over the whole surface of English literature."[12] Their marching orders were explicit:

> Make a quotation for *every* word that strikes you as rare, obsolete, old-fashioned, new, peculiar, or used in a peculiar way. . . .
>
> Make as *many* quotations *as you can* for ordinary words, especially when they are used significantly, and tend by the context to explain or suggest their own meaning.[13]

When one knows how a word has historically been used, and how it typically is used, what more does one need to know?[14]

II.

As distinguished from symbols, *signs* may be characterized as lacking even "a vestige of natural connexion" with what they signify.[15] This has usually been expressed by saying that the sign is arbitrary. There is no real reason why a certain animal should be called a *Hund* on one side of the Rhine River and a *chien* on the other (or a *dog* across the English Channel). With the loss of this "natural connection," the sign appears to have lost any necessary or even rational connection with what it stands for. If there is no reason behind the sign's relation to what it signifies, what then is the basis of its meaning?

One approach to this problem is to deny that signs in fact lack a "natural connection" with what they signify. Examples in support of this view have most often been drawn from *onomatopoeia* and *exclamations*.

With onomatopoeia, sound suggests meaning; natural, physical sounds are reflected in the natural, physical sounds of their word-forms. English *buzz*, *thunk*, *quack*, *gobbledegook*,[16] and Tennyson's "murmur of innumerable bees" are examples. With true onomatopoeia, words have a natural basis for their meaning in the sounds they imitate. It is not simply arbitrary that the word *hiss* means "to make or emit a sharp sound like that of the letter *s* prolonged, as a snake does, or as steam does when forced under pressure through a small opening."[17] But even in the rendering of apparently natural sounds, a considerable residue of the conventional and the arbitrary can often be detected. Why else would the English dog say *bow-wow*, the Scandinavian *vov-vov*, the Japanese *wan-wan*, and the Russian *gaf-gaf?* Similarly, the artistic depiction of common objects varies widely from culture to culture; and even our way of indicating negation or denial by shaking the head is not entirely natural or biologically determined, as shown by the contrary practices in other cultures.[18] Here, as elsewhere, it is not always clear "where 'instinct' ends and 'culture' begins."[19]

Even where conventional, cultural influences are not at issue, the linguistic basis of "natural signs" may sometimes be questioned. "It is generally recognized that words are signs," notes Lévi-Strauss; "but poets are practically the only ones who know that words were also once values."[20] Yet some of the most basic words are seemingly unsuited to carry their "natural" associations. The French poet Mallarmé complained that the phonemic values of *jour* and *nuit* suggest the exact opposite of their respective meanings (presumably reading *jour* as soft, quiet, and languorous; *nuit* as pert, perky, and sprightly).[21] But this is as it should be. If words somehow had to physically resemble what they mean, some of the important "design features" of a modern language—e.g., versatility and flexibility—would be impaired, and many complex or abstract ideas could not be expressed at all.[22]

Exclamations are supposed to reflect the spontaneous, involuntary outpouring of inner feeling and emotion, whether positive or negative. Exclamations are thus regarded as, in some sense, called forth by nature itself and as having a natural basis for their meaning.

> Human speech can be reduced to a fundamental instinct implanted by nature in all living creatures. Violent outcries—of fear, of rage, of pain or joy—are not a specific property of man. We find them everywhere in the animal world. Nothing was more plausible than to trace the social fact of speech back to this general biological cause.[23]

Just as onomatopoeia was viewed as the pure imitation of external sounds, exclamations are seen as the pure expression of internal emotions. But here, too, the influence of culture and convention can often be detected. Why else does the Frenchman exclaim *aïe!* when he hits his thumb with a hammer, while his American counterpart exclaims *ow!*? The influence of particular linguistic systems is even clearer with words conventionally used as exclamations, such as French *diable!* ("devil"), English *damn!*, and a long list of expletives (whose enumeration is left as an exercise for the reader). And in any event, the mere fact of subjective outcries does not explain how exclamations could come to designate or describe objects and thereby convey definite meanings.[24]

Onomatopoeia and exclamations played leading roles in debates over the origin of language extending from Plato's

Cratylus to Darwin's *Origin of Species*. Those arguing for the natural origin of language saw in these "natural signs" the building blocks of an entire linguistic system. Today, however, "natural signs" play at most a marginal role and constitute only a tiny minority of the vocabulary in a modern language. "[L]inguists . . . are agreed that, whatever might have been the case at some earlier stage of man's evolutionary development, in all known languages the connexion between a word and what it stands for is, with relatively few exceptions, arbitrary."[25]

III.

Arbitrariness may be considered a fundamental—perhaps *the* fundamental—characteristic of signs in general and linguistic signs in particular. The term "arbitrary," however, carries a number of different connotations, not all of which may be applicable here: random, without reason, unreasonable, tyrannical, not bound by rules, underdetermined, and so on. The linguist Saussure adds another nuance: "The term implies simply that the signal is *unmotivated:* that is to say arbitrary in relation to its signification, with which it has no natural connexion in reality."[26]

Consider again the example of the blindfolded woman holding a balance as a symbol of justice. Symbols, as previously defined, "show at least a vestige of natural connexion" with what they symbolize and are, according to Saussure, "never entirely arbitrary."[27] Discussing the pros and cons of various possible symbols of justice would not be pointless; we could rationally debate what would do a better or worse job of representing justice. Our reasons would reflect assessments as to how well various features of the symbol conveyed aspects of the concept. Someone might argue, for instance, that the blindfolded woman should be shown peeking out from under her blindfold, since justice is never truly blind. Someone else might argue that the balance should be rigidly fixed in place to symbolize the rule-bound inflexibility of the law, and so on. The point is that there would be a reasonable basis for discussion, "because a symbol has a rational connexion with what it symbolizes."[28]

With signs the situation is different. Consider English *tree*, French *arbre*, and German *Baum*, all of which designate the same object. It would make no sense to discuss whether any of these signs did a better or worse job of designating a tree than any of the others. It is well understood that none of these signs (or any feature of them) attempts, in any way, to resemble any aspect of a tree. As far as representing a tree is concerned, there is no linguistic reason or motive for preferring *tree* over *arbre* or *Baum*. This means that

> there is no issue for the community of language users to discuss. . . . For in order to discuss an issue, there must be some reasonable basis for discussion. . . . But for a language, as a system of arbitrary signs, any such basis is lacking, and consequently there is no firm ground for discussion. No reason can be given for preferring *sœur* to *sister*, *Ochs* to *bœuf*, etc.[29]

This is not to deny that reasons can sometimes be given for preferring one word over another. One might argue for *chairperson* over *chairman* or for *Ms.* over *Miss* and *Mrs.* on grounds that the latter terms are sexist. But that would be a social, political, cultural, even legal argument—not a linguistic one. On linguistic grounds, *chairman* is preferred simply because it is shorter. When faced with lengthy or cumbersome words, the linguistic community typically abbreviates or replaces them. In this spirit, the French government, instead of trying to ban "Franglais" (the French adoption of English terms), might take a critical look at its own official alternatives, e.g. *fin de semaine* for *weekend* and *heures de grande conjoncture* for *prime time.*[30]

Once the English-speaking people adopted, discovered, or invented a numbering system, it must have been evident before long that a word for the number *9* would be needed. The choice of *nine* was arbitrary in the sense that *neuf* or *neun* would, in principle, have served just as well. But once that choice had been made, certain other choices fell into place. Given the series *twenty-one, twenty-two, twenty-three* . . . and the preexisting *nine*, there could hardly have been much choice as to *twenty-nine.*

When the potato was originally introduced into France, there was evidently something of a promotional problem to be solved. The choice of a term for the plant was "inspired to a large extent by didactic considerations," reports Lévi-Strauss; it also reflected "the specific technical and economic conditions which prevailed when this food was finally accepted in France."[31] There was an existing term *pomme*, meaning "apple" but which originally meant any rounded fruit with stone or seeds; a number of variants had already been established in prior usage: *pomme de pin* ("pine cone"), *pomme de grenade* ("pomegranate"), *pomme d'orange* ("orange").[32] And there was also the preexisting term *terre* ("earth"). Voilà: the *pomme de terre!* "Can a choice which has historical, geographical, and sociological connotations, as well as strictly linguistic ones, really be considered arbitrary?"[33]

Lévi-Strauss suggests instead that the term *pomme de terre* "was not prescribed, but existed as a possible solution. . . . The solution is the result of a choice among pre-existing possibilities."[34] The same could be said of the choice of English *twenty-nine.* "[T]he linguistic sign is arbitrary a priori," concludes Lévi-Strauss, "but ceases to be arbitrary a posteriori."[35]

Saussure also distinguishes between "absolute" and "relative" arbitrariness.[36] Absolute arbitrariness is the "basic condition" of the linguistic sign. "For the entire linguistic system is founded upon the irrational principle that the sign is arbitrary."[37] Modern languages as we know them could not function with their characteristic versatility, flexibility, and adaptability if words somehow had to be naturally appropriate to their meanings. Applied without limitation, however, the principle of arbitrariness would lead, as Saussure acknowledges, to "utter chaos"; there is and can be no language in which nothing at all is motivated. Instead, as "a partial correction to a system which is chaotic by nature . . . the mind succeeds in introducing a principle of order and regularity into certain areas of the mass of signs. That is the role of relative motivation."[38]

Perhaps, then, instead of a simple polar opposition between the arbitrary and the motivated, we need to add a third, intermediate category. Thus, words like *pomme* and the cardinal numbers from *one* to *ten* would still be considered purely arbitrary; *hiss* and other examples of true onomatopoeia would still be considered motivated or "naturally" determined. But between these conceptual extremes lies a wide range of linguistic choices affected by symbolic, historical, and meaning-related factors. It may in fact turn out that most of our linguistic system falls into this middle range. (Certainly it is the most important category as far as symbolic speech in the legal sense is concerned.)

Absolute arbitrariness is perhaps most relevant at the earlier stages of language formation and in the naming of new things, e.g. *television*, *computer*, *laser*, *hippie*, *disco*, *Internet*—all of which could have been given any number of other designations. But the great majority of creative uses of signs probably falls in the category of the relatively arbitrary. When one is trying to convey a message by unconventional means—as by symbolic speech—it is particularly important to draw upon and play off the "preexisting possibilities" of a conventional system of signs.

IV.

Suppose you and I are preparing to play a game of chess. We get out the chess board, start setting up the pieces, and then discover that one of my pieces—a Knight—is missing. One can imagine the following dialogue ensuing:

> *Me: Hmmm, it looks like one of my Knights is missing. What should we do?*
> *You: Well, let's see . . . is there anything else you could use instead?*
> *Me: I suppose I could use a coin . . . [checking my pockets]. . . . Darn! It looks like I'm completely out of change.*
> *You: Well, how about a bottle top, a pencil eraser, or something like that?*
> *Me: [Checking around] . . . Hmmm, I don't see anything like that either. What else could I use?*
> *You: [Getting exasperated] Just use anything you like, so long as . . .*

Here I lean forward in anticipation, hoping you will now tell me the minimum physical definition of the chess piece in question, the *sine qua non* of the chess Knight. But let's assume you answer correctly, by which I mean correctly in terms of the minimal functional requirements of a chess piece in the game of chess. In that case, your answer will be of a completely different sort. It will have nothing to do with the Knight at all:

> *You:. . . Just use anything you like, so long as it won't be confused with any of the other pieces!*

In other words, there *is* no "minimum physical definition" of the chess piece in question. Rather, the *other pieces* determine whether a substitute Knight is acceptable or not.

If the physical composition of the Knight were what defined it, then we would not be able to replace it with just anything. But we can—so long as it is sufficiently distinctive to be distinguishable from the other pieces. If you and I were chess grandmasters, we might even just pretend there was a piece where my Knight was supposed to be. I would simply notify you where my invisible Knight "moved." (After all, grandmasters can play entire chess games in their heads.) There is thus absolutely nothing about the Knight itself that is indispensable.

Suppose further that in the course of our chess game (assuming we ever got started) someone wanted to know, "What is the value of a Knight in chess?" In other words, how important to my game is that missing Knight? As is well known, the Knight has a distinctive pattern of moving two squares forward and one square to the side. It is also the only piece that can jump over other pieces. These are the sorts of things I might mention in answering the question about the Knight's value or importance.

But while these are indeed unique properties and functions, it would again be a mistake to concentrate on them to the exclusion of what the other pieces can do. Indeed, a comparison with the other pieces is really the *only* meaningful basis or context for considering the Knight's value. If the other pieces were given broad new powers and their moves changed radically, then obviously my assessment of the Knight's value would have to go down. In short, the question of the Knight's value in and of itself—in isolation from the other pieces—is pointless, if not meaningless.

"Être distinctif, être significatif, c'est la même chose," says the linguist Émile Benveniste.[39] Linguistic signs function much like chess pieces in that they need only be distinctive to do their job. This is a direct consequence of the arbitrariness of the sign. In written language, no particular letter or shape is more aptly suited to express a given sound than any other; they are all measured against conventional functions rather than natural patterns. The shape of the letter *t*, for example, has no necessary or inherent natural connection with the sound it denotes. That being the case, it does not particularly matter how closely individual users of a language conform to the "canonical" written forms of the *t*. There is no standard *Guidebook to Written Language*, with detailed specifications for the shapes of the letters. We are, all of us, continually finding out how well our "version" of written language manages to keep us from being too badly misunderstood.

I can write my *t* pretty much as I please, so long as you can distinguish it from my *l*, my *d*, and so on. I can write my *t* with pencil, pen, or paintbrush; I can carefully calligraph it with a quill pen or chisel it in granite; I can emblazon it on posters affixed to high-speed trains or float it across the sky on helium-filled balloons—so long as I distinguish my *t* from all the other letters, I can make myself understood. At bottom, the question, "How is this letter (supposed to be) written in the language?" is essentially the same as the question, "How successfully does my rendition of this letter make me understood?" The more problems I have in making myself understood, the more closely I should attend to the first question. And the first question simply points to the materials the language provides to help its users make themselves understood. Its problems are their problems.

It is likewise with spoken language. Since no particular sound is more aptly suited to express a given idea than any other (with the possible exception of onomatopoeia), all that matters is the phonetic contrast that distinguishes one sound pattern from another. Saussure remarks on "the latitude speakers are allowed in pronunciation, *provided they distinguish one sound from another*."[40] We are all, in this sense, innovators of our language, continually finding out (particularly in a foreign language) how well our "version" of pronunciation manages to make us understood. (There is no standard *Guidebook to Spoken Language* either.)

It does not particularly matter whether I pronounce the letter *e* with an accent, in a dialect, or in a high-pitched voice, so long as my *e* is distinct from my other vowels. The latitude I have in this regard depends on how or whether my language distinguishes particular sounds. In English, this means I must make *pen* distinguishable from *pin*, *then* from *thin*, *loose* from *lose*, and so on. Fundamentally, the same issues underlie the question, "How much leeway does my language allow me in pronouncing this letter, word, etc.?" and the question, "How far can my pronunciation stray from the mark and still be understandable?" Specific contrasts and levels of contrast are imposed generally by the language, but there is also an "overlay" of my own more or less faithful (and more or less successful) renditions of those contrasts. As a speaker, I am continually negotiating some sort of rapprochement between the two.

Sometimes a language simply does not provide sufficient materials for its speakers to make themselves understood; its problems become their problems. In Germany, speakers are hampered by what would appear to be a serious design flaw in their language: The word for "two" *(zwei)* sounds a lot like the word for "three" *(drei)*. So serious is this problem that some German speakers have taken matters into their own hands and reverted back to an archaic, Old High German form of *zwei*, namely *zwo*, which at least does not sound like *drei*. They are saying, in effect: "Our (official) language does not provide sufficient contrast for successful communication, so we are supplementing the language with some exaggerated (unofficial) contrast of our own." In German dictionaries, *zwo* is listed as "colloquial," with the explanation: "often for better understandability, especially on the telephone."[41]

Likewise, word-forms are arbitrary with respect to their meanings, and for this reason the laws of word-form are simply contrastive and relational. We know that English *thinking* and *thing* are of different forms (even though they nominally share the ending *-ing)*, not because we have systematically memorized all English word-forms but because, parallel to the verb *think*, there is no corresponding verb **th*. *Thinking* fits into a system implied by the relationship between *think* and *thinking; thing* does not. For similar reasons, all of the following are distinguishable as to form, even though they nominally share various endings:

thinker (think)	vs.	*powder (*powd)*
started (start)	vs.	*indeed (*inde)*
higher (high)	vs.	*paper (*pap)*
highest (high)	vs.	*protest (*prot)*
drank (drink)	vs.	*prank (*prink)*
drunk (drink)	vs.	*trunk (*trink)*

In none of these examples is the form itself of importance; or rather, the actual form is important only insofar as it reveals a system of latent relationships.

In inflected languages, nouns are normally declined by means of different endings added to the same stem. But even this degree of formal difference is not absolutely necessary. Sometimes, in fact, the complete absence of an ending can also indicate case. Czech *slovo* ("word") and *žena* ("woman") no longer have positive case endings in the genitive plural. Yet the contrasts *slovo* vs. *slov* and *žena* vs. *žen* work just as well to distinguish these cases. "So it is not even necessary to have any material sign in order to give expression to an idea: the language may be content simply to contrast something with nothing."[42]

In general, all material aspects of language are arbitrary in relation to their meaning; none of them is essential or indispensable. For successful communication, the physical signs of meaning need only be different enough from each other to be distinguishable. A successful system of communication might lack even the sounds of speech. Whether such a system would still amount to a "language" is largely a matter of definition, but John Lyons argues that it would.

> Let us suppose that we were suddenly to discover a society of human beings making no use of vocalization . . . but communicating by means of a complex system of gestures. Let us further suppose that, upon analysis, these gestures were found to have the same kind of grammatical structure (or a grammatical structure of a similar degree of complexity) as our own spoken languages; that they were used for the same or a similar variety of communicative functions, and had various other properties . . . which we think of as being characteristic and distinctive of language by contrast with other semiotic systems. Faced with this hypothetical discovery, we would surely say that the society in question had a language.[43]

The lack of a minimum physical definition of the sign suggests that one should focus primarily on the use or function of signs within a system of communication. If absolutely nothing about the sign itself is necessary for its functioning, then "symbolic speech" (which typically does not use conventional signs at all) takes on general significance as the basic or foundational form in such a system.

V.

Imagine someone—let's call him the Maddening Linguist—who, whenever asked what something was, would give an answer like "Oh, that's what the Germans call *Sauerbraten.*"

You could point to something as simple as a little bird, and he would say, "That's what's known as a *rouge-gorge* in French." If you asked him for directions, he might respond, "A Russian would turn *napravo* at the next intersection." This could get maddening in a hurry, and we would probably come away with the impression that the Maddening Linguist had been of no help at all.

Now imagine someone quite different—let's call her the Helpful Guide—who accompanies you on all your travels abroad. When an agitated Frenchman approaches your park bench, she calmly explains, "He's saying the woman you just kissed is his wife." When a German waiter tries to describe an incomprehensible dish, she cheerily relates, "He says it's made of pigs' intestines and is highly recommended." And so on.

Why would we say the linguist was so singularly unhelpful and the guide so accommodating? The linguist seems to respond only at the verbal level; he answers as a foreigner might, in a foreign language. He gives us merely a foreign-language "label" for what we need to know, whereas the guide really seems to penetrate through to the things themselves.

Yet, in a sense, both the linguist and the guide are merely "translating" their answers from one language to another: in the former case "out of" our mother tongue and in the latter case into it. We just happen to benefit only in the latter case (at the "receiving" end of the transaction), but that has more to do with us and our limitations.

The translations *into* our own linguistic system immediately resonate, so much so that the agitated Frenchman and the incomprehensible German waiter now more or less recede into the background. Once their concerns have been restated in our own idiom, a thousand preexisting lines of interconnection open up, a thousand familiar points of reference emerge. A whole new and more coherent picture starts taking shape immediately with the infusion of this exotic but easily assimilable information.

But with the translations "out of" our language, the exact opposite seems to take place. Etymology can perhaps give us some clues, but otherwise the Maddening Linguist seems only to have contributed a colossal roadblock to understanding. Who would have ever thought that translating something into a foreign language could shed light on its meaning? And yet, if that plan succeeded—if we could come to understand that when the German talks about *Sauerbraten*, he is talking about something like (but also unlike) what we are talking about when we talk about "pot roast". . . we might even end up thinking that *Sauerbraten* is not really much like pot roast at all. But at least the conversation would have been enriched by points of reference beyond the preexisting interconnections of our own familiar idiom (and cuisine). All these subtleties would have been lost had the Maddening Linguist simply said, "Oh, that's just a pot roast" in the first place.[44]

Speakers of a language find themselves somewhere between the situation in which things still need translating and the one in which everything has already been translated. The arbitrary signs of our own language are no more inherently meaningful than those of any other language (we just happen to be more familiar with them). And the categorizations that underlie them may not be the most insightful or helpful either (particularly in a foreign context). All languages function at the interface of two distinctly separate yet continuously parallel realms: one (the realm of thought) is close at hand and intimately familiar; the other (physical signs) is an external, alien, and inherently meaningless medium. Each linguistic system brings these two realms together in a systematic yet totally unique way.

Language, as a system of signification, organizes these realms into two parallel series and establishes correspondences between them. There is a series of units of thought: ideas, concepts, messages. And there is a series of physical signs: in language, the signs are the sounds of speech and the shapes of written letters or characters. (The following discussion proceeds in terms of language—and especially speech—but also applies, as appropriately modified, to symbolic speech and other nonlinguistic systems of signification.)

Each language is uniquely defined by the particular signs it associates with particular units of thought. But languages are even more unique than that. Neither the signs nor the units of thought are predefined or delimited in advance; they too are the unique products of specific social, cultural, historical, and linguistic forces. Thus, underlying each language are *three* unique series of categorizations, which determine (1) how the units of thought are defined; (2) what units of sound are recognized; and (3) which units of thought, as so defined, are associated with which units of sound, among those recognized.

Thoughts

Language

Signs

Language mediates between the realms of pure thought (the subject of philosophy and psychology) and pure sound (the subject of physics and phonetics). But the characteristic role of a language is not simply to supply ready-made units of sound for expressing ready-made units of thought. A better explanation might be that "an idea is fixed in a sound, and a sound becomes the sign of an idea."[45] This formulation suggests that the idea did not fully take shape until it was "fixed" in sound and that the sound in question was not a fully determinate sign until it became *the* sign of a specific idea. One could think of arbitrarily assigned sounds as a convenient way to "mark," categorize, or delimit units in an otherwise amorphous mass of thought. Or one could think of arbitrarily assigned ideas as a convenient way to "mark," categorize, or delimit units in an otherwise amorphous mass of sound. Either way, the creation of units in the one results in the creation of units in the other, since each provides the means for fully determinate distinctions to evolve in the other. As Saussure puts it, "'thought-sound' evolves divisions."[46]

Linguistic units are defined not in terms of their material identity but—rather like the chess piece discussed previously—in terms of their use and role in a system of signification; and each language constitutes a unique and largely incommensurable such system. Why do we say that the 8:45 train from Geneva to Paris is "the same" train as the one twenty-four hours later, even though it has a different locomotive, different cars, different conductor, different staff, and different passengers? We say that because it does the same thing, at the same time of day, on the same tracks, between the same mountains, valleys, and rivers, from the same point of origin and to the same destination—pretty much everything *except* the train itself. Why do we call Zürich's *Bahnhofstraße* "the same" street even after all its cobblestones, pavement, sidewalks, and street lamps have been demolished and replaced with new materials? Presumably because it still functions more or less the same, in the same location, between the same elegant shops and galleries and in the same relationships with all the adjoining streets.

Saussure contrasts these examples with the example of a new suit in my closet. Suppose the suit is stolen and then shows up weeks later (in perfect condition) in a secondhand clothing shop. Of course we say it is "the same" suit (indeed, that would be a legal prerequisite for any efforts to recover it); but here its identity *would* be understood in terms of its material composition (and not in terms of its surroundings, which are not the same).[47]

Linguistic units have the kind of identity that the chess piece, the 8:45 train, and the street have. Their material identity can change, and yet they remain the same. In the course of a symposium, different speakers may pronounce the word *nuclear* with different accents, different stresses, different intonations (or even mangle the pronunciation entirely, as President Bush does with "nucular"); yet it remains the same word—even if these phonic differences are greater than those standardly recognized between *then* and *thin*. The functional identity (or what linguists term the "linguistic value") of *nuclear* persists throughout these permutations because its role in the surrounding vocabulary, subject matter, and context of discussion remains the same. Linguistic identity also does not depend on an exact reduplication of meaning from one use to the next. I can "*adopt* a child" and "*adopt* a fashion" or speak of "the *flower* of the dogwood tree" and "the *flower* of her youth" and still be using the same words each time.[48]

As noted above, each language is uniquely defined by its complementary distinctions and associations of thought and sound. Different languages may occasionally share units of sound, e.g. English *do* (stressed) and German *du* ("you"); but these generally have unrelated roles in different linguistic systems (unless derived from a common source).[49]

The question whether different languages share units of thought is more problematic. Consider again the position of the Maddening Linguist. He seems to be saying that *Sauerbraten* cannot be translated into English. And he may have a point, since American English, at least, has simply adopted the foreign term since about 1885–1890—either because the expression seems uniquely suited to its concept (not likely) or because the culinary item in question seems so uniquely German (more likely).[50] (Better examples of the former possibility might be *joie de vivre* and its brooding Germanic counterpart, *Weltschmerz*.)

But the Maddening Linguist also declined to translate Russian *napravo* ("to the right") or French *rouge-gorge* ("robin"). It seems unlikely (though perhaps still possible) that when a Russian turns "to the right" at an intersection and an American follows in hot pursuit, they are doing anything relevantly different, or even think they are (though the Muslim turning "to the East" to pray may have a better claim to be doing something untranslatable). And presumably if we catch a *rouge-gorge* in France and bring it to America, it would then be called a *robin*. So, does *rouge-gorge* = *robin?*

Translating word-for-word from one language to another would be like using a chess Knight in a checkers game (and expecting it to move as a chess Knight does); or transporting the 8:45 Geneva-Paris train—lock, stock, and barrel—to Grand Central Station in New York (and expecting it to be "the same train"); or relocating all the cobblestones, mortar, sidewalks, and lampposts of the *Bahnhofstraße* to Telegraph Hill in San Francisco (and expecting it to be "the same street"). Word-for-word translation is impossible because of what one has to leave behind: the whole system of distinctions within which the words function and derive their identity—just as, in the previous examples, one had to leave behind the rules of chess, the whole countryside between Geneva and Paris, and the whole district surrounding the *Bahnhofstraße*.

Lyons nicely illustrates the difficulties of translating even something as simple as "The cat sat on the mat" into a foreign language.[51] Even without trying to preserve the rhyme or rhythm, one faces a number of complex choices in French:

"the cat"	"sat"	"mat"
le chat	*s'assit*	*paillasson*
la chatte	*s'est assis(e)*	*descente de lit*
	s'asseyait	*tapis*

In Lyons' example, the meaning of *mat* is limited by its contrastive relations of sense with *rug* and *carpet*. And these do *not* correspond to the contrasts in sense among *paillasson* ("door mat"), *descente de lit* ("bedside mat"), and *tapis* ("small rug").[52]

The meaning of a word is limited in this way by the relations of sense that hold between it and other related words in the same language.[53] *Temps* cannot mean the same thing as *time*, if only because English also has the term *weather*, lacking in French. A word's meaning, observes Lévi-Strauss, "dépend de la manière dont chaque langue découpe l'univers de signification dont relève le mot."[54] True *semantic* equivalence would imply a *cultural* equivalence between relevant objects, situations, and institutions. That equivalence, in turn, would be reflected in equivalent systems of *linguistic* distinctions—both as to distinctions made and distinctions not made. It is highly unlikely that these complementary requirements could ever be met. Systems of signification—and mature natural languages in particular—retain a degree of incommensurability virtually unknown in other social, cultural, and legal institutions.

CHAPTER 4

Boundaries

The previous chapters analyzed key conceptual stages in the expression of meaning. These following chapters apply this analysis to "speech" in the legal context. But before proceeding further, it may be useful to take a look back and a look forward at the same time. What, for example, is special about the legal context in which speech is considered, and how does it differ from the broader contexts of linguistics and philosophy? Do principles drawn from those latter disciplines have any bearing on the legal definition of speech or place legal limits on expression?

I.

Chapter 1 began by distinguishing three basic types of meaning: natural meaning, speaker's meaning, and expression meaning. The remainder of the chapter explored what those different types of meaning have in common. There is, I suggested, a deeper background sense of meaning, in terms of which something can be "meaningful" even if its exact meaning is not known or understood. I called this "contrastive meaning" and illustrated it in a number of different contexts: the scientific discovery of a "natural pattern" amid otherwise meaningless natural materials; the scientific recognition of an intended message amid meaningless background noise; and theories of perception and memory.

Meaning is "contrastive" in the sense that it does not depend on anything inherent in the content of its elements but only on relationships between them. Meaning is not a property *of* things but *between* things, so to speak. This idea has broad implications.

In perception, the "figure" is meaningful only against a "background" that is not significant. Other perceptual contrasts are the interesting vs. the uninteresting and the central vs. the peripheral; if something interesting is on the periphery, this "disequilibrium" is resolved by bringing what is interesting into the center of the perceptual field.

Memory is structured in much the same way. We do not access the past on anything like an "equal opportunity" basis but on a strictly biased basis, determined by what matters most. Our important experiences are not filed away alongside all the relatively mundane events of our lives, as though they were all equally available for recall. Instead, it is precisely the contrast between the important and the (mostly) unimportant that makes the former much more readily available, and thereby allows memory to serve its useful functions (one of which is—I almost forgot—forgetting the unimportant).

This analysis can be extended beyond the two-part relationship of "contrast" to what I called a more general "relational meaning," which encompasses multiple contrasts and levels of contrast. Music is a key example, with melody, harmony, rhythm, and "message" all unfolding at the same time. But, as suggested at the end of Chapter 1, music is still a relatively impoverished purveyor of messages; we have to proceed to symbols, signs, and words for the fullest expression of meaning.

The more detailed analyses of Chapters 2 and 3 trace out the connection between meaning and the means by which it is conveyed. With *symbols* this connection is real and substantial, which suggests both an advantage and a disadvantage. The advantage is the symbol's natural and intuitive relationship with what it symbolizes. The disadvantage is the corresponding limitation of symbols to the concrete and tangible. The skull and crossbones as a symbol of poison, for example, may be about as abstract as "natural symbols" can get.

Chapter 2 explained how a few basic forms of mental synthesis underlie all possible experience of objects in the real world. These forms of mental synthesis (space, time, things, attributes, and causation) are inherently relational; they refer beyond the immediately given data to an implied totality of possible experience. A whole is thereby represented or symbolized in and through each of its constituent parts. Thus, even something so basic as our direct perception of objects in the real world is inherently "symbolic," in that it presupposes and represents a spatial, temporal, relational, and causal continuum (itself not directly experienced) within which alone things can be experienced.

When we pass beyond perception and cognition to the created objects of myth, ritual, religion, art, and other cultural institutions, the role of symbolism becomes deliberate and artificial. Here again, though, the purpose is not to *copy* objective reality but to create contrastive and relational meaning—often more by what is left out than by what is included. Typically, we select, concentrate, and compress a totality of experience into the artistic or religious symbol.

Through symbolism, we thus give form to an otherwise meaningless and inexpressible reality. We single out or compress a total phenomenon into one of its component factors. The particular then represents a universal; it acquires a definite, ideal meaning through its contrast with a totality of possible experience.

The historical transition from symbolism to signification, from natural connections to arbitrary designations, represents the last great stage in the expression of meaning. The *sign* is, at last, freed of any inherent, necessary connection with what it signifies.

Chapter 3 grappled with a key feature of modern language: its "signs" are arbitrary, in the sense that they lack any inherent natural connection with what they signify. Instead of looking beyond or outside a language for indications of its meaning, we must look inside. Linguistic values—like those of the other systems of meaning previously discussed—are contrastive and relational.

Although natural meaning, speaker's meaning, and expression meaning all share a deep contrastive or relational structure, to the extent that they differ it is *speaker's meaning* that predominates in the legal context.[1] Chapter 3 clarified how speaker's meaning arises within an advanced system of signification, especially a language. (Chapter 5 then applies this analysis in legal contexts.)

It may not be an exaggeration to say that the meaning of a sign depends on and is determined by other signs. This is, of course, a somewhat paradoxical way of putting the matter, as it invites the objection of "circularity" (what determines the meaning of those other signs?). But if the meaning of words no longer depends on their connection to nature, it can depend only on their place and role in a system of "non-natural" meaning, created and institutionalized in human language.

A *sign* in the linguistic sense is defined only negatively: it lacks any inherent natural connection with what it signifies. Neither the sign's physical characteristics nor its role within a linguistic system is determined by its meaning as such; indeed, considered in isolation, it *has* no meaning. Instead, the sign's identity and role are functions of a system of signification.

Meaning is conveyed within such a system in a negative, contrastive way too: by distinguishing the sign from other signs, clarifying what it is *not*. The positive richness and fullness of the system itself are presupposed. "At any given period, however far back in time we go, a language is always an inheritance from the past," says Saussure. "In fact, no society has ever known its language to be anything other than something inherited from previous generations, which it has no choice but to accept."[2]

Languages take inherently meaningless sounds and physical shapes and link them up with uniquely defined units of thought. Functional values, not physical characteristics, are what define a language's signs, which are not connected in any necessary way with those of any other language. But *within* a given language, all is not arbitrary; in fact, a relatively small number of linguistic units determines in advance how the completed language must systematically unfold. Creative new uses of language (analogues to symbolic speech) draw upon the preexisting structure of meaning established in such a system.

As newcomers on a preexisting scene, so to speak, we can say something new and distinctive (or, what is the same thing: significant) only by contrasting it with the old, already established, and conventional background.[3] The preexisting relations of sense between and among other, related signs are what give our message its intended meaning, as we draw upon and play off the "preexisting possibilities" of a conventional system of signs.[4] It is thus no accident that "symbolic speech" in the legal sense—conveying a message by unconventional means—consists largely of pointed references to, and contrasts with, conventional forms of meaning. It is new wine in old bottles.

II.

Consider a knock on a door. One dictionary defines *knock* as:

> to strike a sounding blow with the fist, knuckles, or anything hard, esp. on a door, window, or the like, as in seeking admittance, calling attention, or giving a signal: *to knock on the door before entering.*[5]

In the semirural area where I live, one occasionally hears "knocking" sounds caused by tree branches blowing in the wind, falling pine cones, frolicking squirrels, and some seriously misguided birds. One learns to ignore these knocks; they do not mean anything. They are like the meaningless background ignored by the paleontologist and astronomer in Chapter 1.

When someone actually knocks on the door, however, the situation is quite different. But how? How can one ensure that one's knock is meaningful—not the kind to be ignored? What makes a knock a "signal"? Again, thinking back to the paleontologist and astronomer: those trained observers were waiting for some kind of meaningful *pattern* to emerge from against an otherwise meaningless background. Sounds of naturally banging branches, frolicking animals, and misguided birds typically do not form any kind of recognizable pattern; they are random and irregular.

Someone approaches a closed door, unsure whether anyone is inside or whether anyone inside could hear (or understand) a shout. The materials provided by nature are few and sparse: the door, one's hands, and not much else. It is, nevertheless, possible to send a crude signal by knocking on the door, though not just in any fashion whatsoever. Instead, one must offer a contrast with the natural background; one must make a knocking sound that could not have arisen naturally. So one knocks three or four or five times in rapid, regular succession; then one waits awhile and, if necessary, repeats the same pattern. This knocking could hardly be the work of trees, animals, or birds; these knocks are meaningful.

One distinction that emerges from this example is the difference between the natural and the nonnatural. All that was necessary to send a meaningful signal was to do something unmistakably nonnatural. To use the terminology of Chapter 1: The knocking is clearly meaningful, even if its exact meaning is unclear. And although in Chapter 1 the paleontologist was looking for a "natural" pattern, here the sort of meaning we are seeking is, in principle, not to be found in the nonhuman world. (These issues are explored more fully in the next chapter.)

A second distinction emerges from an actual legal case. On June 11, 2007, U.S. Senator Larry E. Craig was arrested in the men's bathroom of the Minneapolis-St. Paul International Airport and charged with disorderly conduct. This charge was based on the following observations of the arresting officer (from his vantage point inside an adjacent toilet stall):

> Craig entered the stall and placed his roller bag against the front of the stall door. . . . From my seated position, I could observe the shoes and ankles of Craig seated to the left of me. . . . At 12:16 hours, Craig tapped his right foot. I recognized this as a signal used by persons wishing to engage in lewd conduct. Craig tapped his toes several times and moved his foot closer to my foot. I moved my foot up and down slowly. . . . Craig . . . moved his

> right foot so that it touched the side of my left foot which was within my stall area.[6]

Apparently, what Senator Craig did is commonly done by those who are in fact seeking sexual contact in such surroundings. And it is not hard to see why. In a toilet stall with only the feet and ankles of nearby occupants visible, what else could one really do to send a (not-too-incriminating) signal?

No natural movements of the feet would serve this purpose, which is to announce intentions and invite a response. In fact, most people are very careful in such surroundings *not* to make any suggestive gestures, precisely so as *not* to signal the corresponding intentions. But for those who do have such intentions, a stylized, artificial, rhythmic tapping of the foot is about as good a signal as can be devised. This is not the sort of thing that would be done accidentally or in the normal course of using a bathroom. It may not be completely clear what is meant (what the toe tapper intends), but *some* message is clearly intended, some game is clearly afoot.[7]

So here we see a second key factor in rudimentary signaling: the signaling of intent. The signaler intends that his intentions be recognized. Without that, there is no point to the signaling, no potential realization of a purpose. But when such a message is successfully conveyed, the recipient recognizes the signaler's intentions; the recipient also realizes he was *supposed* to recognize those intentions. That is the intended "double message," so to speak. (These issues are also explored more fully in the next chapter.)

The American Civil Liberties Union (ACLU) filed an *amicus curiae* brief in the *Craig* case. The ACLU argued as follows:

> Just as the state can make the use of "fighting words"—words likely to incite violence—a crime, it can make the solicitation of an unlawful act a crime. . . . The government may not, however, make the solicitation of a lawful act a crime. . . .

> Sex is a constitutionally protected liberty interest. . . . Thus, the government may make sex a crime only where it has a constitutionally sufficient justification for doing so. . . . The government does not have a constitutionally sufficient justification for making private sex a crime. . . . It follows that an invitation to have private sex is constitutionally protected and may not be made a crime. This is so even where the proposition occurs in a public place, whether in a bar or in a restroom.[8]

The trial court peremptorily dismissed this argument as "inapplicable and potentially misleading" because it relied primarily on an earlier Minnesota decision involving the use of language to commit disorderly conduct, "whereas in the present case, the Defendant is charged under the non-verbal 'conduct' portion of the statute."[9]

But regardless of whether the previous case is on point, or whether Craig was charged under a different subsection of the statute, the fact remains that he was convicted of a crime for something the arresting officer himself "recognized . . . as a signal." In its brief quoted above, the ACLU uses three other synonyms for Craig's conduct: *solicitation, invitation,* and *proposition.* If these descriptions are apt, then the Constitution's protection of speech might fairly be implicated. But just what are the applicable boundaries of "speech" in the constitutional sense? Could they possibly be so broad as to include the tapping of feet in restrooms? And from the fact that certain conduct falls within the constitutional boundaries of speech, does it necessarily follow that the conduct is protected under the First Amendment against all governmental "abridgement"?

III.

For an analysis of the "legal context" in which *speech* is at issue, one might most naturally turn to the development of judicial doctrine. But the history of attempts to demarcate the legal boundaries of speech is mostly a history of failed and inconclusive efforts, as even a brief review will show. Nevertheless, a few helpful clues do emerge.

The following Part examines three legal doctrines that have been used to set boundaries on what counts as speech for constitutional purposes: prior restraints, obscenity, and defamation. Briefly, these doctrines start off by claiming that prior restraints, obscenity, or defamation define what is *not* speech, but, as I shall show, that claim has been unraveled by subsequent judicial decisions in all three areas. So these doctrines do not serve, even negatively, as a definition of speech for legal or constitutional purposes. They do not set the "outer boundaries" of speech.

A.

The Constitution provides that no law shall be made "abridging the freedom of speech, or of the press,"[10] and the boundaries of this prohibition had received some glosses even prior to its ratification. In what were then (and for the next century remained) the most influential and authoritative *Commentaries* on the Anglo-American legal tradition, Sir William Blackstone asserted that

> The liberty of the press is indeed essential to the nature of a free state; but this consists in laying no *previous* restraints upon publications, and not in freedom from censure for criminal matter when published. Every freeman has an undoubted right to lay what sentiments he pleases before the public; to forbid this, is to destroy the freedom of the press; but if he publishes what is improper, mischievous, or illegal, he must take the consequence of his own temerity. . . . Thus the will of individuals is still left free; the abuse only of that free will is the object of legal punishment.

> Neither is any restraint hereby laid upon freedom of thought or enquiry; liberty of private sentiment is still left; the disseminating, or making public, of bad sentiments, destructive of the ends of society, is the crime which society corrects.[11]

In other words, once prior restraints ("*previous* restraints upon publications") such as licensing and injunctions have been removed, "sentiment" and the press are, by definition, free. "[T]he freedom of speech, or of the press" means the absence of prior restraints.

This seemed to be the view of the U.S. Supreme Court in 1907, when Justice Holmes wrote that the "main purpose" of the First and Fourteenth Amendments was "'to prevent all such *previous restraints* upon publications as had been practiced by other governments,' and . . . not [to] prevent the subsequent punishment of such as may be deemed contrary to the public welfare."[12] By 1919, however, Holmes and the Court had acknowledged that "[i]t well may be that the prohibition of laws abridging the freedom of speech is not confined to previous restraints, although to prevent them may have been the main purpose."[13] Later decisions make clear that "immunity from previous restraint upon publication . . . cannot be deemed to exhaust the conception of the liberty guaranteed by state and federal constitutions."[14] After all, as one commentator noted, "the liberty of the press might be rendered a mockery and a delusion . . . if, while every man was at liberty to publish what he pleased, the public authorities might nevertheless punish him for harmless publications."[15]

Today, most controversies involving the constitutional limits of freedom of expression turn on the propriety of subsequent punishment—even in the absence of prior restraints. It would therefore be highly misleading to suggest that the absence of prior restraints somehow defines "freedom of speech" or demarcates the scope or coverage of the First Amendment.

B.

The Supreme Court embarked on a major effort at setting First Amendment boundaries in the important 1942 case of *Chaplinsky v. New Hampshire:*

> There are certain well-defined and narrowly limited classes of speech, the prevention and punishment of which have never been thought to raise any Constitutional problem. These include the lewd and obscene, the profane, the libelous, and the insulting or "fighting" words—those which by their very utterance inflict injury or tend to incite an immediate breach of the peace. It has been well observed that such utterances are no essential part of any exposition of ideas, and are of such slight social value as a step to truth that any benefit that may be derived from them is clearly outweighed by the social interest in order and morality.[16]

This passage is unfortunate; indeed, as Harry Kalven observes, "it has *haunted* constitutional law in more than one later instance."[17] Certainly the implied two-level theory of free speech has raised far more questions than it has resolved. Perhaps the *Chaplinsky* Court meant that the above-mentioned (low-level) "classes of speech" are not among those covered, or originally intended to be covered, by the First Amendment; or perhaps the Court meant that they are not "speech"—within the meaning of the First Amendment—at all. These interpretations would have essentially the same result in any given case; but neither view reflects the Court's considered, contemporary jurisprudence. The following discussion illustrates some of the difficulties that *Chaplinsky's* broad dictum has created.

In the late nineteenth century, prosecutions for obscenity were common. It was generally assumed that the First

Amendment's protections for speech and the press did not extend to obscene material, even if it was expressive in nature.[18] As early as 1878, the Supreme Court had ruled that a federal statute excluding lottery advertisements from the federal mails was not an unconstitutional interference with freedom of the press; the Court made clear that its ruling also applied to other "matter deemed injurious to the public morals," such as "obscene" and otherwise "indecent" publications.[19]

The constitutionality of obscenity laws was first squarely presented in the 1957 case of *Roth v. United States*.[20] Drawing on the two-level theory of *Chaplinsky*, the Court identified the "dispositive question" as:

> whether obscenity is utterance within the area of protected speech and press. . . . All ideas having even the slightest redeeming social importance—unorthodox ideas, controversial ideas, even ideas hateful to the prevailing climate of opinion—have the full protection of the guaranties, unless excludable because they encroach upon the limited area of more important interests. But implicit in the history of the First Amendment is the rejection of obscenity as utterly without redeeming social importance. . . . We hold that obscenity is not within the area of constitutionally protected speech or press.
>
> . . . It is insisted that the constitutional guaranties are violated because convictions may be had without proof either that obscene material will perceptibly create a clear and present danger of antisocial conduct, or will probably induce its recipients to such conduct. But, in light of our holding that obscenity is not protected speech . . . "it is unnecessary, either for us or for the State courts, to consider the issues behind the phrase 'clear and present danger.'"[21]

In other words, obscenity *per se* is outside the protection of the First Amendment; it is thus subject to reasonable regulation, like any other ordinary, constitutionally unprotected activity.[22] Yet as Justice Douglas complained in dissent, "[w]ith the exception of *Beauharnais v. Illinois* . . . none of our cases has resolved problems of free speech and free press by placing any form of expression beyond the pale of the absolute prohibition of the First Amendment."[23]

Roth's two-level doctrine did not last long. In the 1969 case of *Stanley v. Georgia*, appellant Stanley was found in possession of films that were conceded by all to be "obscene." Yet Stanley still received substantial constitutional protection, because "[i]f the First Amendment means anything, it means that a State has no business telling a man, sitting alone in his own house, what books he may read or what films he may watch."[24] In short, "the mere private possession of obscene matter" (unlike, say, illegal drugs, which enjoy no recognized First Amendment status) "cannot constitutionally be made a crime."[25] Thus, not only is obscene speech not beyond the constitutional pale: in some circumstances it may even receive First Amendment protection. Speech does not become "nonspeech" or fall below the radar of the First Amendment simply because it is obscene.

Or at least that would have been the most consistent way to demarcate this particular constitutional boundary. Later cases, it must be said, do not do so quite as consistently, perhaps making obscenity "an instance of that mysterious principle by which the exception proves the rule."[26]

The important case of *Miller v. California* begins by quoting *Roth* to the effect that "obscenity is not within the area of constitutionally protected speech or press," but this was no longer a realistic way of putting the matter in 1973. (Two years earlier in *Cohen v. California* the Court had essentially adopted an "unprotected messages" approach (discussed below) and simply included obscenity on the list of unprotected messages that did not apply in Cohen's case. The messages are "unprotected," to be sure, but they still supply the sort of "content" to which the First Amendment applies.)[27] Instead, the *Miller* Court's own way of putting the matter is, "obscene material is unprotected by the First Amendment"—a standard formulation consistent with the standard view that not all restrictions on speech are unconstitutional.[28] (Indeed, the Court's very next sentence is "The First and Fourteenth Amendments have never been treated as absolutes,"[29] implying—at least—that those amendments apply.) The Court then immediately acknowledges "the inherent dangers of undertaking to regulate any form of expression. State statutes designed to regulate obscene materials must be carefully limited."[30]

Furthermore, when the Court articulates its functional definition of obscenity, prominent on the list of constitutional questions is:

> whether the work *depicts* or *describes*, in a patently offensive way, sexual conduct specifically defined by the applicable state law.[31]

Regulation of the "depicting" or "describing" is regulation of representation, expression, or *speech* in the constitutional sense, which explains the "inherent dangers" of undertaking to regulate it and the need for such regulation to be "carefully limited." Finally, after completing its enumeration of required constitutional limitations on the scope of obscenity regulation, the Court adds, "If a state law that regulates obscene material is thus limited, as written or construed, the First Amendment values applicable to the States through the Fourteenth Amendment are adequately protected by the ultimate power of appellate courts to conduct an independent review of constitutional claims when necessary."[32] None of these concerns and limitations would make sense if the activity being regulated did not count as "speech" in the constitutional sense.

Yet when the Court turns to the countervailing state interests that would justify such regulation, it (1) requires very little by way of justification,[33] (2) defers almost completely to the government's judgment,[34] and (3) views obscenity as enjoying no greater presumption against regulation than other subjects of ordinary legislation.[35] These are usually signs that the regulation in question need only be "reasonable" (not arbitrary or capricious); heightened constitutional scrutiny (normally applicable in First Amendment cases) would then not apply.

The *Paris Adult Theatre* case involved a movie theater that was not open to minors and would not have been entered unaware by unconsenting adults either. ("If viewing the nude body offends you, Please Do Not Enter," read one sign.) Here the Court draws on the work of Alexander Bickel:

> A man may be entitled to read an obscene book in his room, or expose himself indecently there. . . . We should protect his privacy. But if he demands a right to obtain the books and pictures he wants in the market, and to foregather in public places—discreet, if you will, but accessible to all—with others who share his tastes, *then to grant him his right is to affect the world about the rest of us, and to impinge on other privacies*. Even supposing that each of us can, if he wishes, effectively avert the eye and stop the ear (which, in truth, we cannot), what is commonly read and seen and heard and done intrudes upon us all, want it or not.[36]

This suggests the following way of drawing a constitutional boundary around obscenity. If Mr. Stanley invites a few close friends to his home to watch obscene films, that would presumably still be protected. If he asks them to chip in a few dollars for beer and pretzels, that might present a closer case. And finally, if he charges them admission, shows the films on a regular basis, and disrupts the whole neighborhood, then he will have relinquished his right to constitutional protection under the First Amendment. In other words, the "boundary" of obscenity lies between the facts of the *Stanley* and *Paris Adult Theatre* cases.

C.

Libel was another class of speech discussed dismissively in *Chaplinsky;* does its prevention and punishment "raise any Constitutional problem"? In *Near v. Minnesota*—the very case finally limiting prior restraints—the Court thought not: "For whatever wrong the appellant has committed or may commit, by his publications, the State appropriately affords both public and private redress by its libel laws."

> [P]unishment for the abuse of the liberty accorded to the press is essential to the protection of the public, and . . . the common law rules that subject the libeler to responsibility for the public offense, as well as for the private injury, are not abolished by the protection extended in our constitutions. . . . The law of criminal libel rests upon that secure foundation.[37]

Indeed, for nearly a century and a half, the Supreme Court's jurisprudence had "left state criminal libel prosecutions entirely free of federal constitutional limitations."[38]

In *Beauharnais v. Illinois*, the Court brought *groups* consisting of "any race, color, creed or religion" within the protection of criminal libel laws, without perceiving any constitutional problems.[39] Citing the *Chaplinsky* dictum, the Court noted that "criminal libel has been defined, limited and constitutionally recognized time out of mind"; given that laws against such speech directed at an *individual* have been "sanctioned by centuries of Anglo-American law," how can one "deny to a State power to punish the same utterance directed at a defined group"?[40] The Court's conclusion was obviously buttressed by its assumption that

> [l]ibelous utterances not being within the area of constitutionally protected speech, it is unnecessary, either for us or for the State courts, to consider the issues behind the phrase "clear and present danger." Certainly no one would contend that obscene speech, for example, may be punished only upon a showing of

> such circumstances. Libel, as we have seen, is in the same class.[41]

Little more than a decade later, however, those assumptions were definitively put to the test in *New York Times v. Sullivan*, which considered libel "against the background of a profound national commitment to the principle that debate on public issues should be uninhibited, robust, and wide-open, and that it may well include vehement, caustic, and sometimes unpleasantly sharp attacks on government and public officials."[42] Against that background, "libel can claim no talismanic immunity from constitutional limitations," wrote the Court. "It must be measured by standards that satisfy the First Amendment."[43] Indeed, the constitutional guarantees "*require* . . . a federal rule" limiting libel actions by public officials.[44] Later cases made clear that only provably false statements of fact are actionable as defamation,[45] thereby placing the nebulous doctrine of "group defamation" in *Beauharnais* on a decidedly (and probably fatally) shaky basis.[46]

Despite these limitations, *Beauharnais* provides some clues as to the boundaries of the First Amendment. Justice Black notes in dissent that by extending the protection of libel law to "huge groups," the Court changed the nature of criminal libel. The original,

> limited scope of the law of criminal libel . . . confined state punishment of speech and expression to the narrowest of areas involving nothing more than purely private feuds. Every expansion of the law of criminal libel so as to punish discussions of matters of public concern means a corresponding invasion of the area dedicated to free expression by the First Amendment.[47]

One important version of the private/public distinction is the individual/group distinction. The logic justifying sanctions against those who defame individuals no longer holds when relatively large groups are said to be defamed. In *Beauharnais*, the offending leaflet stated: "If persuasion and the need to prevent the white race from becoming mongrelized by the negro will not unite us, then the aggressions . . . rapes, robberies, knives, guns and marijuana of the negro, surely will."[48] How do these "rantings of modern Know-Nothings" (as the Court put it)[49] damage anyone?

> [T]he Illinois legislature may warrantably believe that a man's job and his educational opportunities and the dignity accorded him may depend as much on the reputation of the racial and religious group to which he willy-nilly belongs, as on his own merits. This being so, we are precluded from saying that speech concededly punishable when immediately directed at individuals cannot be outlawed if directed at groups with whose position and esteem in society the affiliated individual may be inextricably involved.[50]

But it is demonstrably harder to defame a group than an individual if defamation is limited to "provably false factual connotations."[51] The statement that "Jones is a liar," for example, "implies a knowledge of facts which lead to the conclusion that Jones told an untruth."[52] By a direct application of the Law of Large Numbers, such knowledge is inherently less plausible about a group than about an individual. The Law of Large Numbers states (very roughly) that an actual outcome, value, or average approaches the mathematically expected outcome, value, or average as the number of instances approaches infinity.[53] "[A]n intuitive way to view the probability of a certain outcome is as the frequency with which that outcome occurs in the long run, when the experiment is repeated a large number of times."[54] As the sample size increases, it becomes more and more improbable that the sample will exhibit extreme—or even distinctive—characteristics.[55]

Jones may well be a liar, and it is easy to imagine the sort of information that could back up that specific claim. But it is hard to imagine what could back up the claim (intended as factual) that everyone of Jones's "race, color, creed or religion" is a liar. Indeed, it would be hard to say *anything* specific—much less defamatory—about all the individual members of such a large group. "Group defamation" begins to sound more like opinion than fact. This is precisely the rationale for removing "huge groups" from the actionable realm of libel law and giving speech about them the protection of the First Amendment.[56]

The *Chaplinsky-Beauharnais* line of reasoning may be reconsidered from yet another angle. The former case had addressed "fighting words" directed to an individual in a face-to-face encounter. It was in this context that the *Chaplinsky* Court considered those words "no essential part of any exposition of ideas. . . . 'Resort to epithets or personal abuse is not in any proper sense communication of information or opinion safeguarded by the Constitution.'"[57]

"Personal abuse" is beyond the First Amendment's boundaries because it has "a direct tendency to cause acts of violence by the persons to whom, individually, the remark is addressed."[58] The statute (as construed) in *Chaplinsky* prohibited only "the face-to-face words plainly likely to cause a breach of the peace by the addressee."[59] The Court's emphasis on the face-to-face context and on the "personal abuse" of an individual suggests two complementary lines of reasoning: (1) people are most likely to fight when provoked by someone within fighting range, and (2) people are most likely to fight when provoked by specific comments about them personally. Under these (and perhaps only these) conditions, the fact that the provocation involves speech is "clearly outweighed by the social interest in order."[60]

According to the *Beauharnais* Court, the Illinois Supreme Court's "characterization of the words prohibited by the statute as those 'liable to cause violence and disorder' paraphrases the traditional justification for punishing libels criminally, namely their 'tendency to cause breach of the peace.'"[61] But the leaflet in question maligned "the Negro," a group comprising many millions of people. Beauharnais's reference to "the aggressions . . . rapes, robberies, knives, guns and marijuana of the negro"[62] cannot be taken as saying anything specific enough about anyone to plausibly provoke anyone (and it would not be face-to-face either). In defamation law,

> general statement[s]—such as . . . a disparaging statement about an entire minority racial group . . . are held not to be actionable by individual members of the group or class in the absence of evidence of special circumstances at the time of publication which reasonably give rise to the conclusion that there is particular reference to a particular member.[63]

Again, by a direct application of the Law of Large Numbers, saying anything specific about individuals as members of groups—whether for purposes of defaming them or of provoking them—is inherently less plausible the larger the group involved.

This larger and more generalized context, moreover, is precisely the one in which important pronouncements concerning public policies and politics typically appear. In *Beauharnais*, noted Justice Black in dissent, "the leaflet . . . was also the means adopted by an assembled group to enlist interest in their efforts to have legislation enacted."

> And the fighting words were but a part of arguments on questions of wide public interest and importance. Freedom of petition, assembly, speech and press could be greatly abridged by a

> practice of meticulously scrutinizing every editorial, speech, sermon or other printed matter to extract two or three naughty words on which to hang charges of "group libel." The *Chaplinsky* case makes no such broad inroads on First Amendment freedoms.[64]

On the basis of this commentary, one can venture some preliminary conclusions about First Amendment boundaries. Clearly, "personal abuse" and "purely private feuds" are afforded little if any protection, even though they might involve speech. But where the speech implicates—even potentially—more general, civic concerns, then the calculus changes. Such concerns are implicated almost by definition whenever "huge groups" of citizens are involved; and "race, color, creed or religion" is an apt classification of some of the most relevant groups. For constitutional purposes, then, one can neither defame nor provoke a group of this magnitude.

IV.

In a recent article aptly entitled *The Boundaries of the First Amendment*, Frederick Schauer usefully distinguishes the question of the *scope or coverage* of the First Amendment from the question of its *protection*. The former question concerns "whether, as a threshold matter, the First Amendment is even implicated at all."[65] The latter concerns "the strength of protection that the First Amendment affords the speech to which it applies."[66]

> Questions about the boundaries of the First Amendment are not questions of strength—the degree of protection that the First Amendment offers—but rather are questions of scope—whether the First Amendment applies at all. . . . [B]oundary disputes [are] disputes not about the protection of the First Amendment, but about its coverage.[67]

The two questions were arguably conflated in *Chaplinsky*, which stated that "fighting words" are "not in any proper sense communication of information or opinion safeguarded by the Constitution."[68] But more recently—and very much in line with the analysis of obscenity and defamation developed above—the Court has finally laid to rest the idea that unprotected speech is necessarily beyond the scope or coverage of the First Amendment. In *R.A.V. v. City of St. Paul*, fighting words are clearly placed within the scope or coverage of the First Amendment, though not within its protection:

> We have sometimes said that these categories of expression are "not within the area of constitutionally protected speech" [citing *Roth, Beauharnais*, and *Chaplinsky*] or that the "protection of the First Amendment does not extend" to them. . . . Such statements must be taken in context, however, and are no more literally true than is the occasionally repeated shorthand characterizing obscenity "as not being speech at all,". . . What they mean is that these areas of speech can, consistently with the First Amendment, be regulated *because of their constitutionally proscribable content* (obscenity, defamation, etc.)—not that they are categories of speech entirely invisible to the Constitution, so that they may be made the vehicles for content discrimination unrelated to their distinctively proscribable content. . . .
>
> . . . It is not true that "fighting words" have at most a *"de minimis"* expressive content . . . or that their content is *in all respects* "worthless and undeserving of constitutional protection". . . ; sometimes they are quite expressive indeed.[69]

More generally, the modern Court has endorsed the view that, within the realm of constitutionally "covered" speech, there are a few (and only a few) distinct categories of "unprotected messages."[70]

> [A]s it comes to us, this case cannot be said to fall within those relatively few categories of instances where prior decisions have

> established the power of government to deal more comprehensively with certain forms of individual expression simply upon a showing that such a form was employed. . . . [W]e cannot overemphasize that, in our judgment, most situations where the State has a justifiable interest in regulating speech will fall within one or more of the various established exceptions . . . to the usual rule that governmental bodies may not prescribe the form or content of individual expression.[71]

Thus, speech may be (1) protected, which means that regulation of its content is presumptively unconstitutional;[72] (2) unprotected, if it falls within one of the few, distinct categories of unprotected messages; or (3) not within the scope or coverage of the First Amendment (and perhaps not really "speech," for constitutional purposes) at all. This last possibility is the one that has not received satisfactory treatment or even discussion.

Schauer focuses on this last issue, but prevailing judicial doctrine and legal analysis provide little guidance. What one would want is a constitutional concept of "speech" that could organize First Amendment analysis the way "seizure" guides Fourth Amendment analysis and "punishment" guides Eighth Amendment analysis. But that is just what is most notably lacking:

> Here the counterpart to "seizure" in the Fourth Amendment and "punishment" in the Eighth Amendment is "speech," a word that is of far less value in setting boundaries. "Speech" is what we use to enter into contracts, make wills, sell securities, warrant the quality of the goods we sell, fix prices, place bets, bid at auctions, enter into conspiracies, commit blackmail, threaten, give evidence at trials, and do most of the other things that occupy our days and occupy the courts. That the boundaries of the First Amendment are delineated by the ordinary language meaning of the word "speech" is simply implausible.[73]

It must be conceded that the boundaries of First Amendment coverage have not been conceptualized in any coherent, intellectually rigorous way. Instead, as Schauer ably shows, whole areas of the law have been included or excluded for reasons having little or nothing to do with their status as "speech." "[T]he boundaries of the First Amendment . . . turn out to be a function of a complex and seemingly serendipitous array of factors that cannot be (or at least have not been) reduced to or explained by legal doctrine or by the background philosophical ideas and ideals of the First Amendment."[74]

In some of the very earliest cases, Justice Holmes simply assumed that "persuasion to murder" and "the counselling of a murder" may constitutionally be criminalized, even though they obviously involve speech. "[T]he First Amendment . . . cannot have been, and obviously was not, intended to give immunity for every possible use of language"; and "neither Hamilton nor Madison, nor any other competent person then or later, ever supposed" otherwise.[75] Indeed, Holmes cites approvingly an even earlier case to the effect that

> In the case of an unlawful conspiracy, the agreement to act in concert when the signal is published, gives the words "Unfair," "We don't patronize," or similar expressions, a force not inhering in the words themselves, and therefore exceeding any possible right of speech which a single individual might have. Under such circumstances they become what have been called "verbal acts," and as much subject to injunction as the use of any other force whereby property is unlawfully damaged.[76]

By what principle or theory are these obvious uses of language placed outside the boundaries of the First Amendment? Schauer suggests a number of factors, most of which (as noted above) have little to do with legal reasoning or constitutional principles. In the context of criminal law, the

First Amendment most often seems implicated "when the defendant's speech is public rather than face-to-face, when it is inspired by the speaker's desire for social change rather than for private gain, when it relates to something general rather than to a specific transaction, and when it is normative rather than informational in content."

> So when Susan whispers to Max that the combination to the office safe is "22 left, 14 right, 37 left," the ability to prosecute Susan for being an accessory based solely on her verbal behavior, even though it is the communication of accurate information to a willing recipient, is unconstrained by the First Amendment because Susan's words are private, informational, specific, and devoted solely to private gain. But when Fred makes a speech to an audience in Central Park urging his listeners to rob banks in order to finance the revolution, the public, noninformational, and ideological nature of this speech brings the First Amendment—specifically *Brandenburg*—into play.[77]

(Note that this does not necessarily mean Fred's speech is protected, only that it is covered, by the First Amendment.)

In summary, there are two distinct issues in setting "boundaries" to First Amendment coverage: (1) whether something is really "speech" at all; and (2) whether something that is conceded to be speech nonetheless eludes First Amendment coverage for lack of "constitutional salience"—the array of "often mysterious political, social, cultural, historical, psychological, rhetorical, and economic forces that influence which policy questions surface as constitutional issues and which do not."[78]

It can hardly be a satisfactory state of affairs for First Amendment theory to turn on "mysterious" or "serendipitous" factors having little to do with legal reasoning or constitutional principles. And in any event, the first issue is the more fundamental; it concerns the necessary (though not sufficient) conditions for something to be salient—for First Amendment purposes—at all. The question, "Is it speech?" serves as a kind of threshold question of constitutional coverage; ultimately, in order to evaluate a First Amendment claim, one must know what "speech" is. Analyzing the coverage of the First Amendment without analyzing speech itself is somewhat like staging a production of *Hamlet* in which Hamlet himself does not appear (or perhaps it is more like *Waiting for Godot*). The following chapters turn therefore to this more basic concern.

CHAPTER 5

Intentions

With the legal context comes a new emphasis on intentions and, above all, on their role in communication. This chapter focuses on the following questions: What does "speech" mean in constitutional, First Amendment law and in ordinary language and the philosophy of language? Under what circumstances does intentional action count as speech? Can communication be unintentional? And what follows (in law) from the fact that almost any action can be made expressive?

These issues may most usefully be addressed first by way of a dialogue with the philosopher Susan J. Brison, whose position is set out in an article entitled *Speech and Other Acts*.[1] Brison stipulates at the outset that

> all speech is conduct, involving an agent, and all conduct, being intentional action, is expressive (of the motivating intention).[2]

This is an admirably broad, abstract proposition—one that might possibly serve as the basis for a philosophical theory of speech (though, as suggested below, I have my doubts); but legal principles are usually developed through the refinement of narrow, case-specific doctrines. While *speech* in the constitutional sense is a term of art, to be defined more precisely in the crucible of judicial reasoning, any usage that simply equates speech with conduct ignores crucial legal distinctions.

There is, of course, a rather elementary sense in which one could proclaim that "all speech is conduct"—the sense, namely, in which speech requires and presupposes some conduct, such as moving one's lips and vocal chords, making marks on paper, and so on. But if "all conduct is expressive," then my dog is expressing herself whenever she barks or even when she chases a squirrel. G.E.M. Anscombe had the best answer to that: "[B]rutes . . . can *have* [intentions], though . . . a cat's movements in stalking a bird are hardly to be called an expression of intention. One might as well call a car's stalling the *expression* of its being about to stop."[3]

From the fact that speech requires and presupposes conduct, we should not conclude that "all speech is conduct," any more than we should conclude that "playing chess is moving pieces of wood." These formulations are inadequate and misleading because they leave out what is most important: the transmission of meaning. For a more plausible theory, the defining scope of *speech* must extend to cases involving communication. Indeed, for purposes of the First Amendment, only speech in its aspect as communication—and conduct that is intended to communicate even if it is not speech in the strict sense—are at issue. As the U.S. Supreme Court has remarked, "To hold otherwise would be to create a rule that all conduct is presumptively expressive."[4]

I.

To the extent that the Supreme Court has a theory of speech, it is the following:

> [1] For "the expression of an idea" to count as *speech*, it must be "sufficiently imbued with elements of communication."
> [2] "An intent to convey . . .
> [3] . . . a particularized message [must be] present."
> [4] "[I]n the surrounding circumstances the likelihood [must be] great that the message would be understood by those who viewed it."[5]

As suggested in the Introduction, the theory must primarily explain communication; and communication entails at the very least a speaker and an audience.

> There is a sense in which everything we do consciously and much of what we do unconsciously is expressive—is the visible counterpart to (or "expression" of) some "inner" mental state, often an emotion such as anger or fear or joy. . . . But the expression that is relevant to freedom of speech . . . is the expression of a thought, sensation, or emotion *to another person*. This is a narrower concept of expression than the first but it is of course enormously broad, encompassing . . . the whole field of human communication, verbal and nonverbal.[6]

The other elements may be viewed as forming a triadic relationship among a speaker's intention to communicate, a relatively specific message, and an audience's potential understanding of that message.

Brison dismisses this theory outright, saying that it "does not succeed in distinguishing speech from nonspeech conduct" and that "it has proven to be notoriously difficult—some would say impossible—for the Court to distinguish speech from other forms of intentional action."[7] But I would not give up so easily. In fact, I shall argue that this account of speech is not just a viable notion for law but also a good one for ordinary understandings of speech and therefore for philosophy too. It provides a starting point.

Consider the following examples:

> *Example 1.* I am asleep in a train compartment, speeding through the European countryside. Another occupant of the compartment takes out a cigar, lights it up, and begins to smoke. As the smoke wafts my way, my nostrils begin twitching, my throat becomes parched, and my resulting cough wakes me up.

For behavior to count as a human *action*, as opposed to a mere event or happening in the physical world, there is a standard philosophical requirement that there be at least one true description of it as *intentional*, as intended by an agent.[8] "If, for instance, Mary is jumping on the sofa and she breaks it, even if she did not break it intentionally, breaking the sofa was her action, because it was intentional under the description 'jumping on the sofa.'"[9] In Example 1, there is no consciousness, no intention, and so no conduct in the sense of intentional action. This cough, Brison agrees, "is not an action, since it is not intentional under any description. It is like snoring or anything else one 'does' while asleep or otherwise unconscious."[10]

> *Example 2.* Now I am awake, and the smoke is still affecting my throat and nostrils. Being very polite and not wishing to disturb anyone, I try not to cough unnecessarily, but eventually it becomes too much and I finally decide to clear my throat with a brief, quiet cough.

(This example is designed to show that intentional action is not necessarily communicative.) This time I coughed on purpose, as everyone normally does when they cough (without, perhaps, thinking about it quite so much). Even assuming this cough sounds exactly like the previous one, here I was not, strictly speaking, *forced* (as in Example 1) to cough; I could have avoided coughing by holding my breath or bolting from the compartment for fresh air. It is true that I meant (intended) to cough, but normally "a cough is just a cough," and I "meant" nothing else by it. In fact, if anything I tried to avoid drawing any particular attention to my plight. So here there is intention and conduct but not (I shall argue) communication or speech.

To return to the distinction between actions and events: Here, coughing is an action and not simply (as in Example 1) an event, since it is intentional under the description "coughing on purpose to clear my throat." (Of course it could also be correctly described as (unintentionally) "contracting certain throat muscles and setting off certain vibrations in the air.") But is it a *communicative* action?

Brison seems to think so: "In deciding not to suppress the cough or leave the room, Y acted in a way that he knew would communicate *something* to X."[11] But think what this would mean. . . . *Every time* someone coughed they would be communicating or "conveying a message," if that was "at least a foreseeable consequence of coughing."[12] In fact, in the example above, *not* coughing would also convey a message—probably even a more obvious one—since I described the alternatives to coughing in pretty dramatic terms ("holding my breath or bolting from the compartment for fresh air"). So, cough or don't cough: either way you can't avoid communicating. Indeed, whatever you do, you will be communicating because this analysis could be extended indefinitely.[13] On Brison's view, it seems that we are pretty much condemned to communicate all the time, whatever we do, so long as someone, somewhere might think it meant something, however unintended. (This issue is important because—as discussed later in this and the following chapter—the distinction between laws related to speech and laws unrelated to speech depends on the prior distinction between communicative intentional action and noncommunicative intentional action. If "all conduct is expressive," then neither distinction can be made.)

Brison supplements this analysis with her own example of yawning "when one has decided not to resist the urge to yawn during a talk that has gone on for too long, knowing (but not intending) that the yawn will signal . . . to the speaker that the talk has gone on too long, whether or not the yawner intends this to be the message communicated."[14] Two issues should be distinguished: (a) Was communication intended? (Here Brison wants to say "No.") (b) Did the actor nonetheless communicate? (And here Brison wants to say "Yes.") For the reasons developed in this chapter, I shall argue that when the first answer is "No," the second answer should be "No," too. But in this particular example, I do not get beyond the first answer, for three reasons.

First, yawning is not particularly difficult to suppress or conceal (unlike the coughing described above). This fact is well known and makes the unsuppressed or unconcealed yawn all the more significant. Second, yawning out of boredom has a long, conventional history, well known the world over and celebrated in stylized depictions since time immemorial in literature, drama, and film. The *Oxford English Dictionary* even defines *yawn* in one sense as "denoting something that induces boredom," and gives as an example: "[They] were very slow in taking the hint conveyed by his violent yawnings, that he was anxious to retire to rest."[15] And third, "knowing (but not intending) that a yawn will communicate something" is implausible (at least in Brison's scenario); it violates the normal presumption that everyone intends the ordinary consequences of their voluntary actions.[16]

> *Example 3.* The smoking continues. Now I am getting a little peeved, and I begin pondering how I might get the smoker to desist. But, still being unfailingly polite, I contrive to do so without causing a confrontation. Perhaps I can help the smoker "figure out" that there is a problem without seeming to complain. So I cough again, this time in hopes of getting the smoker to infer that the smoke is bothering me—and to desist. (Let's assume this cough sounds exactly like the previous ones.)[17]

(This example is designed to show that intentional action—even to influence others' behavior—is not necessarily communicative.)[18] One might say that here I am trying to "plant an idea" in the smoker's mind without wanting the smoker to realize I am doing so. I am hoping the smoker will "get the message," and in that sense I am "sending a message"—but without intending that there be any connection between the two. In fact, I hope the connection will not be evident. If I am successful, the smoker will get the message without realizing I was sending a message.

Normally, however, when we speak or communicate, we do not simply try to plant ideas in people's minds. Or at least, even when that is partly our intention, another part is to "announce our intention" of doing so. Otherwise we would simply be trying to induce changes in behavior as one might with subliminal advertising or in training an animal.

Brison disagrees again; she thinks this example is "analogous to someone's burning a cross on (or right next to) a black family's lawn in an attempt to induce the family to move away" (which would, as she correctly notes, "communicate[ ] a message of terror").[19] But, again, that is a poor analogy. *Everyone* (from the Supreme Court on down) knows that burning a cross is communicative. Practically anything one does to or with a cross means something because the cross is a preexisting symbol with a lengthy religious history. Cross burning itself has a long history and acquired its current meaning of racial hatred more than a century ago:

> Cross burning originated in the 14th century as a means for Scottish tribes to signal each other. . . . Sir Walter Scott used cross burnings for dramatic effect in *The Lady of the Lake*, where the burning cross signified both a summons and a call to arms. . . . Cross burning in this country, however, long ago became unmoored from its Scottish ancestry. Burning a cross in the United States is inextricably intertwined with the history of the Ku Klux Klan.
>
> When D.W. Griffith [made] the movie *The Birth of a Nation* in 1915, the association between cross burning and the Klan became indelible. . . . From the inception of the second Klan, cross burnings have been used to communicate both threats of violence and messages of shared ideology. . . . The first known cross burning in the country [occurred] when a Georgia mob celebrated the lynching of Leo Frank by burning a "gigantic cross" on Stone Mountain that was "visible throughout" Atlanta.
>
> To this day, regardless of whether the message is a political one or whether the message is also meant to intimidate, the burning of a cross is a "symbol of hate."[20]

The point of my example was to test the thesis that "influencing people's behavior is not necessarily communicative," *not* to show that communication can influence behavior (which is easy and which Brison easily shows). Suppose the laws in my jurisdiction make it a crime to "communicate a message of terror" (to quote Brison).[21] As I am puttering around in my yard late one day, I decide to gather up and burn various branches and yard trash that have accumulated there. After I have piled everything into a big heap, some of the branches happen to fall together so as to form a large cross. Thinking nothing in particular about that (other than amusement at the coincidence), I proceed to ignite the pile of debris just as I normally would. Unbeknownst to me, from the perspective of a black family's home not far away, the burning branches show up as a huge flaming cross dramatically framed against the darkening sky. I suppose that "conveying a message . . . was at least a foreseeable consequence" of my actions. So on these facts, according to Brison, I have committed the crime of "communicating a message of terror."[22] (This would be like my Example 2.)

After serving my prison sentence, I return home, determined to seek revenge against my neighbors but equally determined never again to run afoul of the law against "communicating a message of terror." So I secretly release a tiger near the neighbors' house, just to terrorize them. That should certainly succeed in terrorizing them, but the idea that someone did this on purpose—just to "send them a message"—should not be high on anyone's list of likely explanations. (A much more obvious thought would be that the tiger escaped from a visiting circus and just happened to be in the neighborhood, etc.) Yet according to Brison, "[r]egardless of [my] intentions," the release of the tiger "nonetheless communicates a message of terror" to my neighbors.[23] "[I]n spite of the fact that" I do not want them to know that I am "sending a message of terror," I have "terrorize[d]" them, which is apparently enough for Brison to say that I have once again committed the crime of "communicating a message of terror."[24] (This would be like Example 3.)

Example 4. Still the smoking continues and I am losing patience. So I decide on a stylized, ostentatious, highly exaggerated cough that will send an unmistakable message to the boorish smoker:

> Your smoking is bothering me, I want you to know that, I want you to know that I want you to know that, and I want you to stop. "Harrummmphh!"

Now there can be no doubt that I am not "just coughing" but am also, and primarily, "expressing my displeasure." Here, there is communication and perhaps even "speech," at least in the symbolic sense. And here I am not just "sending a message" but am also drawing attention to the fact that I am sending a message. I hope and expect that the smoker's recognition of my intentions will play a role in getting him to stop.

Now the smoker cannot hope to ignore me; or at least ignoring me will mean not just ignoring my cough. It will also mean ignoring the evident fact that I am now intentionally sending a message and expressing my displeasure by coughing.

Brison remains unconvinced. She agrees that this final example is communicative, but she thought the two previous examples were communicative too, so nothing changed with these new facts. The phenomenon of "miscommunication" is supposed to reveal an especially telling objection (to my analysis of Examples 2 and 3 as noncommunicative): "If . . . communicating anything that one does not intend to communicate [were] impossible . . . the everyday phenomenon of miscommunication [would be] impossible."[25]

I am not sure what, if anything, turns on the existence of the word *miscommunication* (or the fact that people say things like "I must have miscommunicated"). I am happy to adopt as my own position the view that "Every miscommunication is itself a communication." The miscommunication does not hit its intended target, so to speak; but it *had* a target. It was simply so poorly and artlessly constructed that someone got not the intended message but a confused or muddled or garbled variant of it—along with the fact (and here there was no mistake) that *some* communication was intended. (The person who says "I must have miscommunicated" does not go on to explain, "I wasn't trying to communicate at all.") So it will not in any way detract from my analysis to consider miscommunication a form or variant of communication. The real puzzle is not how people get the right message but how they know a message is being communicated at all. (Even if this does not seem puzzling for those involved, explaining it is a genuine puzzle.)

II.

It is common ground that there can be communication of unintended meaning. What is subject to debate is whether there can be unintentional communication. Consider the following pairs of sentences:

(1) Someone scored a goal.
The ball passed through the goalposts.

(2) Someone greeted someone.
A greeting took place.[26]

In the description "Someone scored a goal," the ball's passing through the goalposts is being viewed as intentional, as intended by an agent. But for someone to score a goal, the alternative description, "The ball passed through the goalposts" must also be true; and here the ball's passing through the goalposts is being viewed without regard to intention, as a mere event or happening in the physical world. This event could happen in any number of ways (the ball could be lifted up by a bird, perhaps, or by a gust of wind). An ordinary event (a ball's passing through the goalposts) is an action if there is at least one true description of it as intentional (scoring a goal). And in general the actions a person performs intentionally can receive other true descriptions under which they are unintentional.

But now consider the description "Someone greeted someone." Here there seems to be no corresponding event in the physical world that would have to take place in order for "Someone greeted someone" to be true. To add "A greeting took place" sounds redundant or tautologous in a way that "The ball passed through the goalposts" does not. But why? I think it is because with "A greeting took place," no real alternative is suggested; we still are not viewing the greeting without regard to intention, as a mere event or happening in the physical world. Instead, we are importing *intention* into the very concept of a greeting—mainly because it makes no sense to view a greeting "without regard to intention, as a mere event or happening in the physical world." (Would you consider yourself to be "greeted" by a machine or even a trained animal?)[27]

In certain sports and under certain circumstances (e.g., during an actual game and according to the rules), getting the ball to pass through the goalposts *means* you have scored a goal. But suppose that during a game you kick the ball and somehow it passes through the other team's goalposts. That still means a goal was scored (and it was still your action since it was intentional under the description "kicking the ball"), but presumably you did not intend to score a goal for the other team. Could something similar happen in the case of a greeting?

Implied in the idea of a greeting is the intention of remaining on good terms with one's acquaintances—let's call this the "general commitment to friendliness." (This is what the machine and the trained animal lacked; and, indeed, something would be odd about your behavior if you greeted people in the usual ways but then proceeded to be as unfriendly to them as to total strangers.) Since no specific event is required for a greeting, if some event occurs anyway in an unexpected or unintended way, that cannot constitute a "greeting" without the implied intention of friendliness.[28] In this sense, a greeting as such is not susceptible of being described as unintentional. There is thus no such thing as an *accidental* (unintentional) greeting, though someone may of course *mistakenly* think she has been greeted when no one greeted anyone.[29]

Consider the difference between *offending* (which is not necessarily intentional and thus, I shall argue, not necessarily communicative) and *insulting* (which is).[30] The distinction is evident at the terminological level from one of the *Oxford English Dictionary's* examples for *offend:* "Wander they in their pleasing darknesse, offended if you shew them light"; and from its definition of *insult:* "To assail with offensively dishonouring or contemptuous speech or action."[31] The classic bland apology that accepts no blame usually starts out, "I sincerely apologize if I have offended anyone. That was certainly not my intention." This formulation is preferred by politicians and professional athletes who have made some egregious *faux pas* or been caught in especially sordid straits.[32] The idea that they would have wanted to communicate anything (when they did what turned out to be so offensive) is generally the farthest thing from their minds. Deepest secrecy is much more to the point.[33]

Suppose I secretly torture cows in my darkened basement, just for fun. Adherents of the Hindu religion, who consider cows sacred, would no doubt take great offense at this if they were to find out, but I know nothing of that; I am simply pursuing my private hobby. Suppose, however, that secretly filmed videotapes of my cow-torturing rituals arrive (unbeknownst to me) on the shores of India, where the inhabitants proclaim themselves "deeply offended," as indeed they are. But have I communicated anything to anyone?

Irritated by all this controversy and the ominous threats coming my way, I make a special point of inviting to my next cow-torturing event the camera crews of the Indian News Network, with a direct live feed to New Delhi. Now I have truly "added insult to injury," as the saying goes.

For another example, suppose I have (finally) been invited to Madam Rothschild's annual garden party, the social event of the year. Obviously I need a new outfit for the occasion, so I pick out a handsome wool sweater with an abstract design featuring black spots of various sizes on a white background, intermingled with striking red blotches. Unbeknownst to me, Madam Rothschild's beloved Dalmatian Trixie has recently met a horrible fate, crushed by a huge tractor-trailer right in front of Madam Rothschild herself, who was understandably devastated. "The sight of poor Trixie lying there, all limp and bloody," she moaned to all who would listen, "will be with me to my dying day." She forthwith decreed that all images of Trixie should forever be banned from her mansion and grounds.

Imagine my surprise, then, when I make my grand entrance in my striking new sweater. Madam Rothschild, deeply offended, turns bright crimson and practically swoons on the spot—but not before having me forcibly ejected by her security forces. Stung by the injustice of it all, I bide my time, and a year later I get my chance for revenge when Madam Rothschild inadvertently invites me to her next garden party. Now, I already have the perfect sweater to wear this time, for the perfect insult. . . .

An insult is communicative and (assuming it could be the subject of a legal case) counts as *speech* for purposes of the First Amendment. Wearing a certain sweater is not speech in any usual sense; but if it is intended to communicate, it may, under the right circumstances (as in the above example), constitute an insult and count as speech for First Amendment purposes.

The difference between insulting and offending, however, is not simply the difference between intending to insult and not (necessarily) intending to offend. Consider again the cow-torturing example. Some people would probably take offense even at the use of their religion in a (somewhat irreverent) fictional example illustrating legal theory—and that is foreseeable. According to Brison, my use of such an example would be communicative if their offense was "at least a foreseeable consequence" of my action.[34] Does that mean I have also insulted them?

I think more facts would be needed to establish that claim. In general, it would be hard to come up with an example that did not potentially offend *someone*.[35] But specific circumstances could make a given example more than just a potential cause of offense. Perhaps American professors have made a real habit of torturing cows, and the resulting outrage in the Hindu world is well known to all. Perhaps the practice has become such a sore point that even the playful, hypothetical condoning of cow torturing is now (along with, e.g., racism and child molesting) more or less beyond the pale. Under these special circumstances, my use of cow torturing as a casual example could only be a deliberate attempt to dredge up that whole painful history. It would be as if to say, "I know this has been a particularly painful episode for you [since, on my new facts, the outrage is "well known to all"], so *for that very reason* I am going to reintroduce it." What was formerly at most an occasion for taking offense now communicates a deliberate and unmistakable insult.

When I insult you, it is essential that you *recognize* the insult for what it is: a direct communication of ill will from me to you. That recognition is part of the insult. Not only do I want you to feel bad—I also want you to know that I want you to feel bad. And I want that knowledge to be, at least in part, what makes you feel bad. Otherwise, you could feel offended as much as you like, but it might have nothing to do with me or only incidentally relate to me as having provided (perhaps unknowingly) the occasion for your offense. I cannot insult a dog, however much I might want to (even assuming it "distinguishes between being stumbled over and being kicked").[36] And indeed we now have proof that "[w]hen someone steps on your toe on purpose, it seems to hurt more than when the person does the same thing unintentionally."[37]

Paul Grice makes this point with two examples that may at first seem puzzling.[38] First, what is the difference between showing you a photograph of your spouse *in flagrante delicto* and drawing you a picture of the same? (Let's assume the photograph was taken automatically by a security camera.) Once I place the photograph in your hands, it no longer matters whether I or someone else gave it to you or even whether you found it in a drawer. The photograph itself is the best and only necessary evidence; "it does all the talking." But as my drawing slowly unfolds, my (perhaps somewhat mysterious) intentions are at center stage, and even if the resulting picture is identical to the photograph, we would be justified in saying I "meant" something in drawing it that we would not say of my handing you the photograph (unless, perhaps, I do so in an unusually prolonged, suspenseful, dramatic way designed to draw attention to my presentation). The drawing is patterned on something in my mind, which in turn could either closely resemble reality or (unlike the photograph) be completely made up. My evident intention that you believe the former is your only basis for believing it.

Second, what is the difference between a traffic policeman who gestures for me to pull over and one who stands in the middle of the road, blocking my way? In the latter case, I have to stop in any event, whatever the policeman's intentions (just as I would for a cow in the road). In the former case, the policeman gets me to stop only by getting me to *recognize* that he wants me to stop. Suddenly, his gesture *means* something: "Pull over!" (Otherwise I would not pull over.)

The defining characteristic of communication is a certain *transparency of intentions*. The general intention to communicate is understood more specifically as the intention to communicate a particular message. (Where this intention is evident but the underlying message is garbled, we have "miscommunication"; where the intention can be only dimly perceived, we have "doubtful" communication; where it cannot be perceived at all, we have "attempted" (or "failed") communication; and where there is no such intention, there is no attempt to communicate.) And not only are the speaker's intentions recognized (by the audience): that recognition plays a role in fixing the meaning of the message.

So we may analyze "*A* means something by *x*" as implying (1) *A* intends the utterance of *x* to produce some effect in an audience and (2) *A* also intends the utterance of *x* to be recognized (by the audience) as so intended.

> But these intentions are not independent; the recognition is intended by *A* to play its part in [producing the effect] . . . [i.e.,] *A* intend[s] the utterance of *x* to produce some effect in an audience *by means of* the recognition of this intention. . . . Moreover, *A*'s intending that the recognition should play this part implies . . . that he assumes that there is some chance that it will in fact play this part, that he does not regard it as a foregone conclusion that

> the [effect will be produced] in the audience whether or not the intention behind the utterance is recognized.[39]

Thus, the question "How do we communicate?" quickly turns into the question "How do we make our intentions (to communicate) known?" Where there are no established conventions (like those of language) for doing so, we can rely on one of the most basic forms of meaning: contrast.

The significant "figure" on an otherwise plain "background" is, as discussed in Chapter 1, a basic model of contrastive meaning. One of the most useful contrasts for purposes of communication is the contrast between the natural and the "nonnatural." Doing something in a natural, normal, functional way is not likely to draw any particular attention to its character as a potential communication.[40]

Suppose I am lost in the wilderness, hiking alone without any supplies. I want to signal which way I have gone to anyone who might be following me or trying to rescue me. There is not much to work with. But supposing I have been prescient enough to bring along my trusty *Boy Scout Handbook*, I could flip to page 160 and read: "Trailing is the ability to follow the deliberately made trail marks arranged by one outdoorsman for another to follow."[41] All well and good, but how does one make a trail mark?

> *Scout trail signs* are scratched in the ground with the point of a stick or shaped from twigs or pebbles. A small arrow means "This is the trail."[42]

Still, one can easily imagine terrain where arrows scratched in the ground might be difficult to discern. Not to worry—there are also *Indian trail signs:*

> The Indians made their signs by placing small stones in certain ways or by knotting grass into small tufts or by pushing sticks into the ground.[43]

The key to making trail signs is suggested by a common difficulty in following them: "When you follow a trail made up of trail signs . . . [b]e sure that each sign is actually a sign and not one you are just imagining."[44] One of the Indian trail signs is a small rock placed on a larger one, with a third rock to the side (indicating a turn in that direction). It is conceivable that one rock could end up on another in the natural course of events, making this sort of sign inherently doubtful. Another Indian sign consists of a stick leaning on another stick (lodged in a notch or fork) and pointing in the intended direction. This too could conceivably happen by accident. If one had some rope or string, one could improve the clarity of the sign by lashing the stick to a tree, preferably with a straight end pointing the way and a forked end suggesting the feathers of an arrow. That would not be mistaken for anything purely natural, but it still could be the remnants of some man-made, functional device other than a sign, such as a simple ladder or shelter. So it would be even better if one had a hammer, nails, lumber, and saw with which to cut out a large, stylized arrow and nail it prominently to a tree. Now *this* trail marking is clearly (1) contrastive with its surroundings, (2) nonnatural, (3) nonfunctional, and (4) indicative of its maker's intent.

A hiker looking for trail signs is like a detective looking for clues. The sign draws attention to itself as something that does not "belong" in the natural order, something not of that order, something artificial that "stands out" as such. More specifically, it stands out as something that was deliberately put in place for a purpose, something expressing an intention. The viewer who correctly interprets the sign also comes to a startling realization: "I was *supposed* to recognize an intention here; those things were arranged just so that I would come to that realization." The sign means what it does just because of that realization.

In Examples 2 and 3 above, coughing in the normal way did not communicate. But upon hearing the stylized, ostentatious, highly exaggerated cough in Example 4, the boorish smoker could only wonder, "Now, why would anyone cough like *that?*"—unless, perhaps, the cougher was trying to do something more than just cough—that is, trying to send a message by coughing. In doubtful or ambiguous cases, "one way for an actor to indicate that otherwise noncommunicative conduct is being used to convey information is to do the act in such a way as to show that it is obviously not meant to perform its ordinary function, and indeed, that the act is done for no evident noncommunicative reason at all."[45] If you drive toward me at night with your lights off, I might turn my lights off and on rapidly. Seeing that, you might wonder: "Now, why would he do *that?*—unless, perhaps, he is trying to signal me that . . . oops! My lights are off."

But where we have established conventions for communication, these elaborate mechanisms for ensuring the recognition of intention may no longer be necessary.[46] When I use the turn indicator on my car (in the usual way), it means "I am about to turn," and it already includes the implied intention to communicate that fact (and to turn). But suppose I want you to know that the sun is shining. I might invite you into my office, lead you to the window, open the shades, and gaze out into the sunlight myself—all in hopes of getting you to see and realize that the sun is shining. But none of this is equivalent to *telling* you: "The sun is shining." Indeed,

> I have performed no communicative act at all. I have arranged things so that you are very likely to end up believing that the sun is shining. But . . . [i]f I *tell* you that the sun is shining . . . I intend that you recognize my intention to get you to believe that the sun is shining.[47]

Included in the conventional use of language is the implied intention to communicate. With a true act of communication I share my intentions with you, and your recognition of those intentions is an essential element of what I intend.[48]

III.

A siren sounds. What does it mean? (This is like asking about *expression meaning* or perhaps *utterance meaning*.)[49] How does it mean what it means? And by virtue of what does it mean what it means?

When I was growing up in Memphis, Tennessee, air-raid sirens sounded every Saturday at noon, so precisely and regularly that you could almost set your clock by them. These sirens meant, "We're just testing the sirens." If the sirens had sounded at any other time (and I am pleased to report that they never did), they would have meant: "This really is an air raid. Take cover!"

This situation may be formally analyzed as follows:

> In the case of a simple signal, a noncomposite whole-utterance-type *x* that means *p* in *G* [a group of people], the theorist can say that the meaning-determining feature of *x* is that there is a practice in *G* of uttering *x* and meaning thereby that *p*. . . . [T]hat practice is precisely the feature of *x* which members of *G* exploit . . . when, in uttering *x*, they mean that *p*.[50]

As for sirens they are, first of all, not something one would likely use unless one intended to send a message. Second, a well-known practice (policy, habit) has grown up around the use of sirens, such that they are used primarily as a kind of warning signal (though in North America their use is so infrequent that their meaning arguably derives more from stipulation or agreement than from any "practice").

Obviously, sirens occasionally need to be tested, but, just as obviously, the populace is going to be extremely confused (and upset) if it cannot distinguish a real warning from mere testing. The consistent practice of testing the sirens (only) at noon every Saturday solves this problem. What is, in effect, a nonnatural, nonfunctional use of the sirens enables them to communicate something beyond the primary message of warning.

In law, symbolic speech corresponds to simple signals, which "have sentence-like meaning, but whose meanings are in no sense determined by the meanings of any of their constituent parts."[51] (This analysis of simple signals does not extend to whole sentences of a natural language. A competent speaker of a natural language knows what novel sentences mean, sentences that have never been uttered before or perhaps [say, because of their length] never *could* be uttered. That knowledge could not have been derived from a preexisting practice, at least not one that associated particular meanings with particular sentences.)[52] The meaning of a simple signal develops out of a consistent practice; and as more people learn about the practice, the more it has that meaning.[53]

As suggested in Chapter 1, an *utterance* (of an expression) shares features with the *expression* of which it is an instantiation on a particular occasion, and with the *speaker's meaning* (and intentions) that the particular act of utterance presumably reflects.[54] What is the meaning of an utterance? Is it the meaning of the expression uttered or simply what the speaker meant in uttering it?

In the case of symbolic speech, the best answer might be: a little of each. Suppose (to use an example suggested by Michael Moore) "actor *A* stands before an audience, twirling his fingers in a clockwise motion."[55] Asking "What did *A* mean by that?" is obviously just another way of asking

"What were *A's* intentions?" Instead, says Moore, the question should be directed at expression meaning: "what does *that* (the twirling of the fingers) mean?"—and to this there seems to be no satisfactory answer.

> To inquire into the meaning of this act is seemingly to ask only for the intentions of the actor *A*. . . . [C]ommunicative acts that are *A's* invention have no meaning, even though *A* meant something by them and even though an audience understanding *A's* intention, could understand what he meant.[56]

Yet Moore also acknowledges that "[a]ctions such as *A's* 'have meaning' precisely because actions are done with intentions, as traditions as diverse as Freud, Weber, and ordinary language philosophy recognize."[57] *A's* actions have contrastive or relational meaning, as discussed in Chapters 1 through 3; what they lack is *conventional* (expression) meaning.

> If actions of this *type*, twirling the fingers clockwise, are generally understood to mean, "it is time for dinner," then to ask for the meaning of *A's* act may be construed as asking for the meaning of [this] *type* of action. . . . [58]

The process by which a practice can give rise to meaning—where previously there was none—may be analyzed as follows. Suppose (to use an example suggested by Stephen Schiffer) a speaker (*S*) wishes to convey to an audience (*A*) that he is angry.[59] Perhaps conditions are so primitive that there is no established language; but suppose it is common knowledge in the group (*G*) to which *S* and *A* belong that "grrr" resembles the sound that dogs make when they are angry.

As Chapter 3 makes clear, sounds may be turned into meaningful "signs" but not by virtue of any inherent properties of the sounds themselves: whether a sound has meaning cannot be determined simply by hearing it. A sound that is highly significant in one society may be meaningless in another. Whether a sound means something depends on the *use* that is made of it. So suppose *S* utters "grrr," hoping that *A* will infer (at least in part from knowing that "grrr" resembles the sound dogs make when they are angry) that *S* is angry. And suppose *A* correctly makes this inference.

Does "grrr" now mean "I am angry" in *G*? At this point, the situation is not that different from the one in which a *dog* makes the sound "grrr" (which would presumably be a good basis for inferring that the dog is angry). Schiffer argues that even if members of *G* "frequently or always" use "grrr" in this way, it still does not necessarily mean "I am angry,"

> for we could still conceive of its being the case that on each occasion that a member of *G* means that he is angry by uttering "grrr," he intends the relevant feature *f* of "grrr" (from which the audience is to a large extent expected to infer that by uttering "grrr" the utterer meant that he was angry) to be the fact that "grrr" resembles the sound dogs make when they are angry.[60]

In other words, the message is conveyed not by a direct recognition of the speaker's intentions but by the audience's making a reasonable inference, aided in this case by a natural resemblance (as discussed in Parts I–II above). Schiffer argues further that for "grrr" to be the same as "I am angry," "this feature *f* must not be one that is true of ['grrr'] independently of people meaning something by uttering ['grrr']."[61] The feature of "grrr," that it resembles the sound that dogs make when they are angry, does not meet this condition because it is true whether or not people mean something by uttering "grrr."

What could meet this requirement? Suppose that in uttering "grrr," *S* relies not on the natural resemblance between "grrr" and the sound that dogs make when they are angry (in order to encourage the inference that he, *S*, is angry), but on the fact (assuming it is a fact) that members of *G* "have meant or mean or have agreed to mean" that they are angry by uttering "grrr."[62] *This* feature of "grrr" has nothing to do with a natural resemblance; this feature points directly to the *use* of "grrr," not its properties. The difference is the difference between the recognition of a resemblance and the recognition of an intention. This feature relates "grrr" much more directly and specifically to the speaker's intention to communicate that he is angry.

"Grrr" has been used by members of *G* to indicate that they are angry. Originally it had a natural basis in resemblance, but now it is simply "their way" of indicating that they are angry. Knowledge of this practice reinforces its utility; the more widely it is known that "grrr" has been used to indicate that one is angry, the more useful it will be for that purpose; and thus it is even more likely to be used, which in turn makes it even more widely known, and so forth. When this process has finally culminated in "an overt or public *acceptance*" or adoption of "grrr" as a means of communicating that one is angry, then one may say that "grrr" means "I am angry."[63]

Analytically, where the speaker's intention was originally to call attention to a *resemblance*, the speaker's intention now is to call attention to a *practice* (of calling attention to a resemblance). The resemblance provided the basis for an inference; calling attention to the practice prompts direct, specific recognition of what the utterance "grrr" has been used for, namely to indicate that the speaker is angry.

> *Ex hypothesi*, *A* managed, with difficulty, to guess that *S* uttered "grrr" intending thereby to communicate to *A* that *S* was angry. The difficulty *A* had in figuring out what *S* was up to was due to *A's* not having prior knowledge of what *S* believed he could accomplish by uttering "grrr."[64]

But once this "prior knowledge" is in place, *A* can directly recognize *S's* intentions. The prior knowledge of *S's* practice serves as a surrogate or substitute or "proxy" for *S's* own announcement of his intentions. The speaker's reference to the practice incorporates and implies an intention that the speaker's intention (to convey that he is angry) itself be recognized, just as it would be if the speaker himself were to say, "I am angry."

The same process of substitution can be analyzed from the speaker's perspective as well. Initially, *S* might think, "If I utter 'grrr,' maybe *A* will infer that I am angry (at least in part from knowing that 'grrr' resembles the sound that dogs make when they are angry)." But after this use of "grrr" has become an established practice, *S* might simply reason, "I shall utter 'grrr' if I intend *A* to think that I am angry." Given sufficient awareness of the practice or policy of uttering "grrr" to communicate that one is angry, *S* can expect *A* to think, "*S's* policy is to utter 'grrr' with the intention that the audience should think he (*S*) is angry. So, since *S* has uttered 'grrr' now, with the policy in force, I take it that *S* is angry."

But uttering "grrr" with these expectations as to the audience's response (where the expectations are reasonable) is the same as uttering "grrr" with the reasonable expectation that the audience will recognize the speaker's intentions (and will take "grrr" to mean "I am angry," at least in part by recognizing the speaker's intention that it do so). It is the same as if the speaker had said, "I am angry," which conventionally carries the implication that the speaker's intentions will be recognized. With a simple signal (e.g., "grrr"), the *practice* of using the signal this way carries the same implications. So *S* can utter "grrr," with the intention that the audience should think *S* is angry; given the practice of uttering "grrr" in such circumstances, *S* now *means that* he is angry, because the audience recognizes (from the practice) *S's* intention that the audience think *S* is angry.[65]

Reference to the practice now serves as a kind of stylized shorthand for what was originally a laborious process of inference. Now "grrr" can be used in all sorts of situations, even ones where the original inference might not have been made. In fact, it is no longer even necessary to know that "grrr" resembles the sound that dogs make when they are angry. (That can be left to the etymologists and philologists.)

Symbolic speech subsists at the interface between meaningful actions that have no generally recognized meaning (because there is no established practice of using them to mean anything) and the generally recognized messages they can eventually convey (once such a practice is established). In this way, mere utterance meaning (and the speaker's meaning and intentions supporting it) can, under the right circumstances, eventually attain the same sort of objective, intersubjective status as expression meaning.

IV.

The foregoing parts of this chapter have argued for an intention-based theory of speech. The key to developing this theory is the analysis of symbolic speech (communication by nonlinguistic means). Since symbolic speech lies at the constitutional boundary between speech and nonspeech, determining what constitutes speech in the case of symbolic speech amounts to a minimal definition of "speech" in the general case. The theory thus provides a general definition of speech that applies even (indeed, even more so) in clear cases involving language. The essential elements of the theory may be summarized as follows:

1. Nonnatural Meaning
2. The Signaling of Intent

3. The Recognition of Intent
4. Establishing a Convention

Nonnatural Meaning

There is such a thing as "natural" meaning: for example, a pattern (say, bilateral symmetry) in a fossil. This pattern is meaningful (to certain scientists, at least) against the background of mostly random rocks and shards from which it emerges; but it is not communicative. No one is trying to send a message here, and no message is recognizable as having been sent.

The Signaling of Intent

What makes a knock on a door meaningful and also communicative? Like the fossil pattern, it contrasts with a neutral background (in this case, silence). But precisely because it could not have been accidental (unintentional), it draws attention to itself as a potential communication. The knocking forms a pattern that nature would not have created; and creating nonnatural meaning is the preeminent communicative task—the more nonnatural, the better. (Philosophers have risen to the occasion here, with examples featuring everything from pound notes thrown out of windows to severed heads served up on platters.)

The Recognition of Intent

Knocking on the door of an empty house is not communication. (There must at least be a potential occupant even if there is not an actual one.) To complete the picture, we must shift to the perspective of the audience.[66] The audience understands the message so long as it also understands two further, formal conditions: (1) the message is intentionally being sent to the recipient; and (2) the fact that the message is intentionally being sent to the recipient is intended as common or mutual knowledge between the sender and the recipient (so that each knows it and each knows that the other knows it). If there is a very avaricious man in my house and I throw a pound note out of the window to get him to leave, does that *mean* something like "You should go"? No, because "I did not intend his recognition of my purpose to be in any way effective in getting him to go." ("If, on the other hand, I had pointed to the door or given him a little push," it might.)[67]

Establishing a Convention

Convention is established by usage—or better: the knowledge of usage. Faced with a meaningful but novel bit of intentional action, we might understand it in terms of the actor's evident intentions; but that is not the same as understanding an expression itself. For that, we need a little help from precedent. Suppose x has been used by a speaker to mean p and has been so understood by an audience. The knowledge that by using x the speaker has been understood to mean p now gives the speaker a reason to use x in order to mean p; and it likewise gives the audience a reason to so understand and interpret x. "Because it has worked, it becomes established; and then it works *because* it is established."[68]

V.

The Supreme Court's jurisprudence of "symbolic speech" provides instructive variations on the meaning of simple signals. These cases typically require a demarcation of the boundary between speech and conduct or between expressive and nonexpressive activity. So in most of these cases, the first issue is, "Is this 'speech' at all?"

Sleeping

Since actual sleeping is by definition not conscious or intentional activity, the only interesting question would be whether activities surrounding the fact of sleeping or "going to sleep" might be considered expressive. If the ordinary, functional, natural action of sleeping were "speech," then the term would (as in Brison's usage) lose all significance. Only under special circumstances can sleeping be considered expressive. What might those be?

The Supreme Court faced this question in the case of *Clark v. Community for Creative Non-Violence* (CCNV).[69] Respondents CCNV wanted to camp and sleep in tents on the Capitol Mall to dramatize the plight of the homeless.

According to the Court, "a message may be delivered by conduct that is intended to be communicative and that, in context, would reasonably be understood by the viewer to be communicative."[70] The burden on CCNV would be to create a "special context" in which sleeping—normally only a natural, functional activity—could be brought into connection with other elements and be seen in a new light, as communicative. This involves bringing together elements that mean more together than they do separately. "[T]he context in which a symbol is used for purposes of expression is important, for the context may give meaning to the symbol."[71]

The chosen location on the Capitol Mall serves this purpose, as it is traditionally used for demonstrations and protests and is not normally a place for sleeping. The use of tents, instead of the real houses most people live in, and the focus on sleeping, which for the homeless is a constantly unmet need, all combine to make for a "remarkably apt fit between the activity in which respondents seek to engage and the social problem they seek to highlight."[72]

On the other hand, the burden would also be on CCNV to show that the sleeping it wanted to showcase was something more or other than the normal, functional activity. The Court points out that

> although we have assumed for present purposes that the sleeping banned in this case would have an expressive element, it is evident that its major value to this demonstration would be facilitative. Without a permit to sleep, it would be difficult to get the poor and homeless to participate or to be present at all. This much is apparent from the permit application filed by respondents: "Without the incentive of sleeping space or a hot meal, the homeless would not come to the site."[73]

This also makes sense of the fact that "the Government . . . appl[ies] its absolute ban on sleeping yet is willing to allow respondents to engage in activities—such as feigned sleeping—that [are] no less burdensome."[74] Feigned sleeping would be more clearly expressive because it would not simply fulfill the ordinary, nonexpressive need for sleep. The "symbolic speech" of feigned sleeping represents a more significant and conspicuous departure from normal, functional activities; it counts as more communicative and should therefore receive greater constitutional protection.

Flag Burning

In one of the early flag-burning cases, Justice Fortas stated:

> If a state statute provided that it is a misdemeanor to burn one's shirt . . . on the public thoroughfare, it could hardly be asserted that the citizen's constitutional right is violated.[75]

This is correct as far as it goes; the case for shirt burning (as opposed to flag burning) as protected communication or "speech" would be difficult to make because the shirt lacks any preexisting symbolic significance (except perhaps in connection with "the shirt off my back"). As explained in Chapter 3, it is beyond the ability of any individual to establish or institute meaningful conventions or linguistic traditions *de novo;* we always find ourselves in a preexisting linguistic and symbolic system that is not of our, or anyone in particular's, making. As things now stand, the shirt has only a natural or functional significance.

But in a continuation of his argument, Justice Fortas indicates (probably inadvertently) how that might begin to change:

> [And if] the arsonist asserted that he was burning his shirt . . . as a protest against the Government's fiscal policies, for example, it is hardly possible that his claim to First Amendment shelter would prevail. . . .[76]

Perhaps; but this is precisely how the shirt burner would be advised to proceed: to bring his novel symbolism into more familiar usage with established protest conventions, perhaps through clever combinations of the "shirt off my back" slogan and complaints about onerous and oppressive taxation. As the shirt-burning movement gradually moves into the mainstream, it will no longer be so easy to say that nothing is expressed or communicated by burning one's shirt.

Likewise, there is nothing particularly communicative about burning a few pieces of wood. But once they have been arranged into the form of a cross, a connection with established symbolism is immediately obvious. Yet this could not have been established all at once by any particular person or even a group; instead, the usage and practices that evolved over time are what gradually bestowed on cross burning its current meaning. In *Virginia v. Black*, the Court traces out a lengthy history of cross burning, starting in the fourteenth century.[77]

The symbolism of flag burning followed a similar pattern. In *Smith v. Goguen*, the appellee wore an American flag sewn to the seat of his pants, thereby making at least a fashion statement.[78] But there is also some preexisting symbolism surrounding the seat of one's pants, not only as to undesirable outcomes but also as to what gets sat on, smushed, disgraced, and otherwise maligned (presumably all captured in the expression "Sit on it!"). At about the same time, in *Spence v. Washington*, the appellant, as part of an antiwar protest, affixed a peace symbol to an American flag, thereby combining two symbols with established meanings in a novel and suggestive form, rich with unmistakable new connotations.[79] Moreover, in the context of nationwide antiwar protests, "it would have been difficult for the great majority of citizens to miss the drift of appellant's point at the time that he made it."[80]

In *Texas v. Johnson*, respondent Johnson went to a great deal of trouble to bring his flag-burning protest within the "context" of the 1984 Republican National Convention.[81] He did not create his symbolism out of whole cloth either, but he did help bring the elements together. And some of the work had already been done for him: inside the convention hall, delegates were wildly waving American flags and generally draping themselves in the patriotic symbolism of the flag, all for the benefit of a national television audience. At his trial, Johnson explained his "communicative" strategy as follows:

> The American Flag was burned as Ronald Reagan was being renominated as President. And a more powerful statement of symbolic speech, whether you agree with it or not, couldn't have been made at that time. It's quite a just position [juxtaposition]. We had new patriotism and no patriotism.[82]

After the decision in *Texas v. Johnson*, Congress promptly enacted the Flag Protection Act of 1989.[83] After enumerating all the things that may not be done to the flag, the Act also states:

> (2) This subsection does not prohibit any conduct consisting of the disposal of a flag when it has become worn or soiled.[84]

As is well known, the proper way to dispose of a worn or soiled American flag is to burn it respectfully and ceremoniously (presumably so it does not end up in a garbage dump).[85] What better way, then, to ensure the protected expressive status of flag burning, than to specify (but then exempt) the only known normal, functional, nonexpressive way to burn a flag!

Nude Dancing[86]

The case of nude dancing is a little different.[87] There a plurality of the Supreme Court concluded that "nude dancing of the kind sought to be performed here is expressive conduct within the outer perimeters of the First Amendment, though we view it as only marginally so."[88] Behind this unilluminating pronouncement lay a difficult calculus. In the lower court, Judge Richard Posner had just issued an amazing opinion that forcefully tied vast swaths of art, music, and even literature to the fate of the lowly striptease dancers in the Kitty Kat Lounge.[89]

One can sympathize with the Justices' reluctance to become drama critics or theater reviewers. But it should not be overly difficult to make the required distinction between, say, a production of *Hair* (which involves nudity) and the striptease dancing at the Kitty Kat Lounge. One might usefully begin with the plurality's own description of the latter:

> The dancers are not paid an hourly wage, but work on commission. They receive a 100 percent commission on the first $60 in

> drink sales during their performances. Darlene Miller, one of the respondents in the action, had worked at the Kitty Kat for about two years at the time this action was brought. Miller wishes to dance nude because she believes she would make more money doing so.[90]

What does nude dancing *mean?* What is the dancer's intended message, and what message does the audience receive? Let us say, charitably, that the message is an erotic feeling; when it is successfully evoked and conveyed, the audience has that erotic feeling. But the audience's recognition of the dancer's intentions seems to play no essential role in coming to have that feeling. The audience is stimulated by the nude dancer, not by the nude dancer's intentions (if any). Perhaps, with the requisite intention (of communicating an erotic feeling), the dancer does a better and more stimulating job than if the audience were voyeurs or Peeping Toms secretly watching her undress in her apartment; but even that is unclear. (Some might consider this the more erotic experience.) Posner places great emphasis on the striptease as preparation for an imagined sexual encounter:

> [O]f course nudity and disrobing are not invariably associated with sex. The goal of the striptease—a goal to which the dancing is indispensable—is to enforce the association: to make plain that the performer is not removing her clothes because she is about to take a bath or change into another set of clothes or undergo a medical examination; to insinuate that she is removing them because she is preparing for, thinking about, and desiring sex.[91]

I am reliably informed, however, that—for some—the medical examination is the perfect setting for a sexual encounter. *De gustibus non est disputandum;* on that we can all agree. The audience may indeed recognize the dancer's deliberate attempts to be erotic; but the recognition of that intention is not what makes her erotic. She is erotic anyway, with or without the recognition of her intention.

Two things should be distinguished here. Nude dancing is "expressive"—it is the outward manifestation of an inner intention, an intention the audience can recognize.[92] But nude dancing does not represent the communication of (nonnatural) meaning. For that, the audience's recognition of the dancer's meaningful intentions would have to be instrumental in conveying her message.[93] To be sure, the audience derives plenty of "meaning" from the nude dancer and her performance; but this is probably the sort of "natural meaning" described in Chapter 1. Even if the dancer wiggles so as to make herself more enticing, she still is not pointing beyond herself to some further message.

As discussed earlier,[94] presenting someone's severed head on a platter does not *mean* something like "This person is dead," even if the audience would easily conclude as much, and even if the audience recognizes that this is the intended conclusion. The fact that the audience would "easily conclude as much" anyway, makes the recognition of the intention more or less irrelevant. The case of nude dancing is analytically the same: The dancer intends to be erotic and presents herself as such. The audience easily finds her erotic, for the full and sufficient reason that she seems erotic—partly, no doubt, as a result of her deliberate efforts to appear erotic. But the audience need not take into account the intentions behind those efforts in order to find her erotic.

The nude dancer is essentially showing something (herself) to someone (the audience). In simply showing something one does not, properly speaking, mean something (unless, perhaps, the showing itself is done in an unusual way that draws attention to the shower's intentions, which then would have to be taken into account).[95] Showing something to someone and letting that person draw inferences or conclusions is not communication.[96] If every time I needed to tell you about something I could only show it to you, meaningful communication would be fatally impaired. Telling is an *alternative* to showing—an abstract, symbolic alternative. I can tell you in words what something *would* look like if I showed it to you; I can paint a verbal picture of it, and I can tell you many, many things that I could not possibly show you.

As in another example discussed above,[97] my drawing of a picture for you *means* something only if your recognition of my intentions plays a role in fixing that meaning. Drawing the picture for you then reveals some further message or implication, something for which the picture is "evidence" but which goes beyond the evidence when you recognize my intentions. Nude dancing, by contrast, is like the case of my giving you a photograph instead of drawing the same thing for you. Now, whatever my intentions (you could just as easily have come across the photograph in a drawer), the photograph itself provides the "best evidence" for your inferences or conclusions, and my intentions add nothing. So we would not properly say I *meant* anything in giving it to you (unless, again, my presentation of it necessarily draws attention to my intentions).

The nude dancer simply reveals the evidence. The audience may appreciate this evidence (and indeed the dancer's efforts in revealing it are part of the picture, so to speak), but the dancer does not mean anything *further* in revealing it (unlike, say, a performer in a production of *Hair*, which has a plot of sorts or at least some themes). Here there is no theme to be furthered, no plot beyond the revealing itself. (At best, the theme is, "Will the dancer be fully revealed—and when?!") The resulting, fully revealed evidence does not point beyond itself to some further message or implication. (In fact, if it did, the audience's experience might be diminished or diluted.) In this sense, "the medium is the message."[98]

Posner states at one point that "[t]he pitter-patter of raindrops does not become expressive activity by being recorded,"[99] and certainly in the usual case rainfall, whether recorded or not, does not constitute meaningful communication. But one can imagine cases in which rainfall (or recorded rainfall) could be used to make a meaningful point; and in that sense showing something—however meaningless—can be put to the service of a larger narrative. For this, one would need to draw the audience's attention to what is usually taken for granted, to encourage the hearing of old things in new ways. John Cage has plenty of ideas along these lines:

> Wherever we are, what we hear is mostly noise. When we ignore it, it disturbs us. When we listen to it, we find it fascinating. The sound of a truck at fifty miles per hour. Static between the stations. Rain. We want to capture and control these sounds, to use them not as sound effects but as musical instruments. . . . Given four film phonographs, we can compose and perform a quartet for explosive motor, wind, heartbeat, and landslide.[100]

Something analogous could conceivably be done by the nude dancer, if there were a larger theme the nudity enhanced. Posner sees such a theme in "erotic emotion":

> Though there is no striptease without some stripping—in today's moral climate, without a great deal of stripping—the dancing and the music are not distractions from the main theme, patched on to fool the censor; they are what make a given female body expressive of a specifically sexual emotion. The striptease is the ensemble of the music, the dance, the disrobing, and the nude end state; it is more erotic than any of its components; and what makes it more erotic than the body itself, or the disrobing itself, is, precisely, that it is *expressive* of erotic emotion.[101]

But, as noted above, something can be "expressive" without conveying (nonnatural) meaning. For the latter, the dancing and disrobing would have to be done in new and unusual ways to draw attention to the disrobing dancer's (or is it dancing disrober's?) intentions; as it is, there is no need to see things in new ways—the audience is apparently quite content to see things in precisely the old, usual, and expected ways. Indeed, it is notoriously insistent upon this point. "In a real barroom," notes Judge Cudahy, "messages would probably also flow in the opposite direction, in the form of encouraging comments to the performer from the patrons. . . . *E.g.*, 'Take it off; take it off!'"[102] Are the patrons missing Posner's "larger narrative point" (which makes striptease "a narrative quite as elaborate as that found in pantomimic ballets (such as *Romeo and Juliet*) and more elaborate than the narratives in wordless music"[103])? Or is this perhaps the patrons' way of saying there *is* no larger narrative point? (One might as well say that the "plot" in juggling is whether the performer will drop any of the balls.)

A further implication of true communication is that the message should be freely recognized—not causally produced by natural, functional forces. Getting people to do, think, or believe something is not in itself meaningful communication.[104] If I start throwing pound notes out of my window to get you to leave,[105] you might initially wonder whether this is some sort of signal (meaning, e.g., "You should leave"). But if I escalate to £1,000 notes, you will probably not stick around (or care) to find out why, but instead run out to pick up some of those £1,000 notes for yourself. (Who could afford not to?)

In the trail marking example previously discussed,[106] suppose that instead of scratching arrows in the ground to signify "This is the way," I simply set out big, juicy hamburgers every few hundred yards. The famished, lost hiker following me can be expected to follow the trail of hamburgers, whether or not he recognizes any intention on my part to signal "This is the way," and perhaps even if this clearly is *not* the way. Likewise in the case of nude dancing: for the appreciative audience, the nude dancers are not like trail signs; they are like big, juicy hamburgers!

So, it is no dishonor for nude dancing to be placed on the list of entertaining but noncommunicative diversions. The Supreme Court has already placed social or recreational dancing on such a list.[107] Other courts have included nude sunbathing.[108] Judge Posner, citing Professor Wright, refers to

> a vast gray area populated by street performers who swallow swords or walk on glowing coals or guess people's ages or weights, by people who wish to make a "statement" by dressing outlandishly, by creators of video games, by contestants in dance marathons, and so on without end.[109]

And for his part, Professor Wright concludes that "[e]xpressive entertainment in the form of juggling, plate balancing, and the swallowing of swords or goldfish . . . however captivating, [is] simply not speech."[110] The meaningful things are what usually get overlooked, and the world—and the law—are poorer for that; but one must also guard against finding meaning where there is none.

CHAPTER 6

Descriptions

Now, what about the objection: "Any action can be made communicative. Therefore it is impossible for courts to distinguish speech from other forms of intentional action."[1] Here is a more elaborate version:

> Consider laws imposing criminal sanctions for the defacement of public property. Such laws do not "bring the First Amendment into play"; a defendant accused of defacing a city bus would not have a First Amendment defense. This would be true regardless of whether the defacement took the form of random blotches of color spray-painted onto the walls, or the form of words like "Down with Clinton" or "Eric is Cool" carved into the seats. Although in the latter case the defendant has satisfied the *Spence* test—his words carry a particularized message that is likely to be understood by his audience—no court in the country would consider the case as raising a First Amendment question.
>
> This example can be multiplied indefinitely, for any action can at any time be made communicative in a manner that satisfies the *Spence* test.[2]

This objection correctly implies that one and the same action can be viewed either as expressive or nonexpressive, depending on the actor's intentions and the surrounding circumstances. But it does not follow that this leaves courts unable to make principled distinctions or to determine that certain conduct, though it could be described as expressive (and thus indeed counts as "speech"), is nonetheless *not* (constitutionally) *protected* speech.

In the passage quoted above, Robert Post asks whether the First Amendment is brought "into play" (or whether "a First Amendment question" is even raised) as a way of asking whether something comes within the *scope* or *coverage* of the First Amendment. If it does, then the further question as to constitutional *protection* can be pursued.[3]

Even though these underlying doctrines have not been worked out in detail, this two-step approach can potentially simplify and clarify First Amendment analysis. First, the issue of coverage must be addressed; that was the subject of Chapter 5. The minimal but general theory of speech developed there (in the context of symbolic speech) specified the necessary conditions for constitutional coverage, i.e., for counting as "speech" for First Amendment purposes. Likewise, the *Spence* Court first found it

> necessary to determine whether [Spence's] activity was sufficiently imbued with elements of communication to fall within the *scope* of the First and Fourteenth Amendments, for as the Court noted in *United States v. O'Brien* . . . "[w]e cannot accept the view that an apparently limitless variety of conduct can be labeled 'speech' whenever the person engaging in the conduct intends thereby to express an idea."[4]

The *Spence* Court then plunged into a lengthy discussion of "the communicative connotations of the use of flags." "[T]here can be little doubt that appellant communicated," noted the Court; as in the armbands case, his display of the flag with a superimposed peace symbol "conveyed an unmistakable message."[5] The question "Is it speech?" may thus be viewed as a threshold question of scope or coverage.[6]

After expression or expressive conduct has been found to come within the scope or coverage of the First Amendment, the issue as to whether it is constitutionally *protected* can then be considered. That is the subject of the present chapter. In *Spence*, after concluding that it was confronted with "a case of prosecution for the expression of an idea through activity," the Court then turned to the task of "examin[ing] with particular care the interests advanced by appellee to support its prosecution."[7] Likewise in *O'Brien*, the Court noted that "even on the assumption that the alleged communicative element in O'Brien's conduct is sufficient to bring into play the First Amendment, it does not necessarily follow that the destruction of a registration certificate is constitutionally *protected* activity."[8] These clearly are questions of protection, and the following discussion proceeds on this basis.

I.

As an initial matter it may be useful to distinguish cases in which (1) the problem addressed by legislation is "independent of the message being regulated," and those in which (2) the problem "arise[s] from the particular dangers of the message being conveyed."[9]

An example of the first would be *Kovacs v. Cooper.*[10] In that case, Kovacs used a sound truck "to comment on a labor dispute then in progress" in Trenton, New Jersey.[11] He was convicted under the following ordinance:

> [I]t shall be unlawful . . . to play, use or operate for advertising purposes, or for any other purpose whatsoever, on or upon the

> public streets, alleys or thoroughfares in the City of Trenton, any device known as a sound truck, loud speaker or sound amplifier, or radio or phonograph with a loud speaker or sound amplifier, or any other instrument known as a calliope or any instrument of any kind or character which emits therefrom loud and raucous noises and is attached to and upon any vehicle operated or standing upon said streets or public places aforementioned.[12]

At the trial, a city patrolman testified that he "located" Kovacs's sound truck by "going in the direction of said sound."[13] (One infers that the sound was loud.) Kovacs "admitted that he . . . spoke into the amplifier."[14]

Several possible descriptions of Kovacs's action can be gleaned from this brief description of the facts:

> Kovacs commented on a labor dispute.
>
> Kovacs made a little speech.
>
> Kovacs spoke into an amplifier before an audience.

All of these descriptions would seem to implicate core First Amendment concerns and call for the most searching judicial scrutiny of Kovacs's subsequent conviction.

But the facts of the case—and especially the ordinance—suggest other possible descriptions as well:

> Kovacs made "loud and raucous" noises.
>
> Kovacs used or operated a sound truck.
>
> Kovacs disturbed a Trenton neighborhood.

These are not normally the sorts of things that raise First Amendment concerns; but they are precisely the sorts of things we would expect a city to do something about—in the exercise of its police powers—to enhance its citizens' welfare and perhaps even their safety.

The Supreme Court was well aware that the first sorts of descriptions could apply, but it upheld Kovacs's conviction anyway. The Court viewed Trenton's ordinance as addressing a problem that was "independent of the message being regulated"—namely, the problem of *noise*. Sound trucks make a lot of noise, regardless of the message being communicated or whether a message is even communicated at all. As John Hart Ely put it, "the values the state seeks to protect by such regulation, values of quiet and repose, would be threatened as much by meaningless moans and static (which is usually how it comes out anyway) as by a political message."[15] The problem of noise does not "arise from the particular dangers of the message being conveyed"; noise is harmful "even if no one sees an expressive element in it." By contrast, *speech* can lead to trouble "only if people know what it means."[16]

To be sure, speech is noise too, but the availability of both descriptions cannot make either description privileged or controlling to the exclusion of the other. Instead, a better formulation might be:

Speech = noise + meaning

Or perhaps (to paraphrase Ezra Pound), one could say that speech is "noise charged with meaning to the utmost possible degree."[17] Focusing exclusively on either the noise or the meaning sheds no light on the constitutional problem.

In *Kovacs*, the relevant question is not what Kovacs was doing but what Trenton was doing in enacting the ordinance. The issue is not whether Kovacs's use of the sound truck counts as speech or nonspeech (it counts as both), but whether Trenton's ordinance counts as a regulation of speech or not. To all appearances, the city was simply addressing the problem of noise:

> The avowed and obvious purpose of these ordinances is to prohibit or minimize such sounds on or near the streets since some

> citizens find the noise objectionable and to some degree an interference with the business or social activities in which they are engaged or the quiet that they would like to enjoy.[18]

New Jersey law granted to its municipalities the authority "to prevent disturbing noises," and the Court notes that on business streets the "distractions" posed by sound trucks "would be dangerous to traffic at all hours useful for the dissemination of information."[19] In residential neighborhoods, "the quiet and tranquillity so desirable for city dwellers" would likewise be threatened.[20] On this basis, the Court concluded that "the need for reasonable protection in the homes or business houses from the distracting noises of vehicles equipped with such sound amplifying devices justifies the ordinance."[21]

This justification does not depend on any consideration of the messages conveyed by sound trucks. The dissenters in *Kovacs* argued that a ban on sound trucks "can give an overpowering influence to views of owners of legally favored instruments of communication," such as the press and radio (to which one would no doubt add television today).[22] But the record was apparently devoid of any specific evidence that any such favoritism played any role in Trenton's deliberations on the subject. Sound trucks may indeed be the "poor man's printing press,"[23] but as Justice Frankfurter put it in concurrence:

> So long as a legislature does not prescribe what ideas may be noisily expressed and what may not be, nor discriminate among those who would make inroads upon the public peace, it is not for us to supervise the limits the legislature may impose in safeguarding the steadily narrowing opportunities for serenity and reflection.[24]

II.

In the important Warren Court case of *United States v. O'Brien*,[25] David Paul O'Brien burned his draft card on the steps of the South Boston Courthouse in 1966 before a "sizable" crowd, to protest the Vietnam War and the draft. At the time, draft card burning had become a familiar form of protest against the Vietnam War and the draft. Everyone knew what it meant. (Indeed, "[i]mmediately after the burning, members of the crowd began attacking O'Brien."[26]) Thus, when O'Brien burned his draft card, what he did could be described as follows:

> O'Brien protested the draft and the war by burning his draft card.
> O'Brien communicated a message of opposition to the draft.

By burning his draft card O'Brien also ran afoul of the following federal law (newly amended as italicized):

> [An offense is committed by any person] who forges, alters, *knowingly destroys, knowingly mutilates*, or in any manner changes any such [Selective Service registration] certificate.[27]

On this basis one could also describe what O'Brien did as follows:

> O'Brien intentionally caused the physical destruction of his draft card.
> O'Brien impeded (somewhat) the smooth functioning of the Selective Service System.

These are of course just the sorts of descriptions that would justify the law. Starting with the constitutional power of Congress to "raise and support Armies" and to make all laws "necessary and proper" to that end,[28] it would be difficult to gainsay the Court's explanation that "[t]he issuance of certificates indicating the registration and eligibility classification of individuals is a legitimate and substantial administrative aid" that "substantially furthers the smooth and proper functioning of the system that Congress has established to raise armies."[29]

But these worthy interests and the descriptions of O'Brien's conduct to which they apply in no way alter or diminish the *other* descriptions of O'Brien's conduct as expressive and communicative. Nor does the Court hold otherwise; it "assum[es] that the alleged communicative element in O'Brien's conduct is sufficient to bring into play the First Amendment."[30]

Recourse to the elusive speech-conduct distinction is tempting but unavailing. What O'Brien did is, as Ely nicely puts it, "an undifferentiated whole, 100% action and 100% expression."[31] The descriptions of "what O'Brien did" as *speech* are in no way incomplete, inadequate, or misleading; nor are the descriptions of what he did as *conduct*. Both sets of descriptions fully, accurately, and correctly characterize what O'Brien did, each in its own terms.[32] There is no sense in which one could somehow choose between them, so that his "speech" would be protected while his "conduct" would be subject to regulation.

III.

The *O'Brien* case involved *symbolic speech:* O'Brien burned his draft card to make a point. He used no words, language, or actual speech. The *Kovacs* case, however, involved the prohibition of a medium of speech. At the time he was arrested, Kovacs was speaking (into a microphone) about a labor dispute.

According to the Court (and under current doctrine), symbolic speech is at issue "when 'speech' and 'nonspeech' elements are combined in the same course of conduct."[33] In *O'Brien*, the "speech element" was the message of opposition to the war and the draft that O'Brien communicated by burning his draft card. The "nonspeech element" was O'Brien's physical destruction of his draft card and his presumed disruption of the Selective Service System.

But there was a "nonspeech element" in the *Kovacs* case too: noise. That noise got Kovacs in trouble under Trenton's ordinance. And indeed the Court was satisfied that noise *alone* got Kovacs in trouble—not his speech or "speech element" or message.

Without making at least *some* noise, Kovacs could not have communicated anything at all by speaking. All speech has a physical basis.[34] In other words, all speech—not just "symbolic speech"—combines "'speech' and 'nonspeech' elements . . . in the same course of conduct." If, by speaking very loudly and noisily, Kovacs had destroyed a draft card, then he would have done so by means of "nonspeech elements," just as O'Brien did.

"Content-neutral" regulations of speech (like the one at issue in *Kovacs*) are reviewed today under a relatively deferential and forgiving standard of review—a form of intermediate scrutiny. Relatively deferential review is appropriate when, as the Court has put it, "there is no realistic possibility that official suppression of ideas is afoot."[35]

Symbolic speech is also reviewed today under a form of intermediate scrutiny—at least when it passes the test set out in *O'Brien*.

> [T]he four-factor standard . . . for validating a regulation of expressive conduct . . . in the last analysis is little, if any, different from the standard applied to time, place, or manner restrictions.[36]

This is no coincidence. "Content-neutrality" is just another way of saying that legislation, regulation, or prohibition addresses only "nonspeech elements." But if the statute at issue in *O'Brien* had explicitly banned "draft-card burning as a form of protest against the Vietnam War and the draft," then it would have done what the Court was confident had *not* been done in the *Kovacs* case (or in *O'Brien* itself): erected a content-based barrier to speech.

IV.

In *O'Brien*—paralleling *Kovacs*—the relevant constitutional problem is not how to characterize what O'Brien did but how to characterize what Congress did. The issue is not whether O'Brien's burning of his draft card counts as speech or conduct (it counts as both), but whether Congress's statute counts as a regulation of speech or of conduct.[37]

"[W]hen 'speech' and 'nonspeech' elements are combined in the same course of conduct,"[38] writes the Court, a special new test is called for:

> [A] government regulation is sufficiently justified [1] if it is within the constitutional power of the Government; [2] if it furthers an important or substantial governmental interest; [3] if the governmental interest is unrelated to the suppression of free expression; and [4] if the incidental restriction on alleged First Amendment freedoms is no greater than is essential to the furtherance of that interest.[39]

Obviously, criterion [3] is of special concern in the *O'Brien* case, and the Court devotes considerable discussion to it. "We note at the outset that the 1965 Amendment plainly does not abridge free speech on its face, and we do not understand O'Brien to argue otherwise. . . . It prohibits the knowing destruction of certificates issued by the Selective Service System, and there is nothing necessarily expressive about such conduct."[40] Despite the valid descriptions of

O'Brien's conduct as communicative, the fact that the government's preferred descriptions are equally valid shows, again, that "there is nothing *necessarily expressive* about such conduct."[41] It can be described in a way that makes it communicative; but it can also be described in a way that makes it noncommunicative. Thus, the Court is satisfied that "both the governmental interest and the operation of the 1965 Amendment are limited to the noncommunicative aspect of O'Brien's conduct. The governmental interest and the scope of the 1965 Amendment are limited to preventing harm to the smooth and efficient functioning of the Selective Service System."[42]

Well, not exactly. The statute is not "limited" so as to prevent the abridgment of O'Brien's expressive conduct. It simply addresses conduct that could *also* be described as noncommunicative. In other words, the statute is limited to conduct that is not "necessarily expressive."[43]

Conduct that is "necessarily expressive" would presumably be conduct that could be described *only* as expressive. As an example, the *O'Brien* Court mentions the case of *Stromberg v. California*.[44] There, the Court struck down a statutory phrase that punished "[a]ny person who displays . . . any flag, badge, banner, or device . . . as a sign, symbol or emblem of opposition to organized government."[45] Clearly, the statute singles out expressive activity for punishment; but the underlying action by which one "displays" a flag could also be described in nonexpressive terms ("moving a piece of cloth on a pole," etc.). So the issue is not whether a certain communicative action can also be described as noncommunicative (it always can be). The question is, rather, whether the conduct *defined in the legislation* can fairly be described as noncommunicative. If the statute at issue in *Stromberg* had expressed concern solely about, say, the safety hazards involved in "moving a piece of cloth on a pole," then that would have made for a very different case. Then, the fact that some *other* conduct covered by the legislation could be described as communicative (e.g., waving a flag) would not stand in the way of upholding the statute.

In *Tinker v. Des Moines School District*,[46] decided just nine months after *O'Brien*, high school students were suspended for wearing black armbands to protest the Vietnam War. Despite the apparent similarity to *O'Brien*, the Court treated this summarily as "the type of symbolic act that is within the Free Speech Clause of the First Amendment . . . closely akin to 'pure speech' which, we have repeatedly held, is entitled to comprehensive protection."[47] But *Tinker* would have been a very different case (and presumably would have followed *O'Brien*) "had it arisen, for example, in the context of a school regulation banning armbands in woodworking class along with all other sartorial embellishments liable to become safety hazards."[48]

Two things should be distinguished here: (1) the difference between actual conduct (in the real world) and the "ideal conduct" defined in a statute; and (2) the multiple descriptions to which the former (but not the latter) may be subject. Actual conduct (in the real world) can often be described both as expressive and nonexpressive. As explained in Chapter 5, expressive conduct (or "speech" for constitutional purposes) is a special kind of intentional action that requires and presupposes an underlying physical basis. In this sense, all speech is also conduct, but not all conduct is speech. Thus, all expressive conduct can also be described as nonexpressive, but not *vice versa;* nonexpressive conduct can (also) be described as expressive only under certain conditions and in certain special circumstances.

The most useful perspective for understanding the case law is not that of actual actions (which, if they are expressive, can always be described as nonexpressive too) but of the "ideal conduct" defined in a statute. This ideal conduct is already being viewed as either expressive (communicative) or nonexpressive (noncommunicative)—but not both. It comes complete with its own (basis for) interpretation, namely, the terms of the statute, its legislative history, and all other relevant circumstances surrounding its enactment.

Once an event in the real world occurs, it is subject to various (true) descriptions from various points of view. But the "ideal conduct" defined in a statute never actually occurs. It exists only to the extent that it is defined (and in that sense described), and its definition is formulated from one particular point of view. The subject of legislation is defined (and already understood), for example, *as* speech or *as* conduct but not both. The details that might have given rise to other descriptions are left out; those factual details do not exist, so they cannot form the basis for alternative descriptions. The lawmaker is addressing a future that has yet to unfold, and all we know about the measure adopted in legislation is what the legislature has told us about it.

The statute represents only one "version" of the future; it is in that sense partial or incomplete—a fiction.[49] (Likewise, people may disagree as to how Hamlet's moods should be interpreted; but those same people should agree that all we know about Hamlet is what Shakespeare has told us about him. That—despite the disagreement—is the one and only valid basis for determining what *Hamlet* means. An actual historical figure, by contrast, can and should be interpreted in light of the total historical record.)

It follows that when noncommunicative conduct is clearly the target of legislation, that conduct cannot (also) be viewed as communicative. Legislation inevitably leaves itself open to challenge, however; because of its generality, *other*, unanticipated actual conduct may emerge that both falls within the legislative prohibition and is also clearly expressive (as in

CCNV—the case involving sleeping as a form of protest—and, arguably, *O'Brien*). But this will not necessarily invalidate the legislation (as *CCNV* and *O'Brien* show).[50]

But now suppose that conduct, *as defined in legislation*, cannot fairly be described as noncommunicative. The statute at issue in the important flag-burning case of *Texas v. Johnson* read as follows:

> (a) A person commits an offense if he intentionally or knowingly desecrates:
>
> 1. a public monument;
> 2. a place of worship or burial; or
> 3. a state or national flag.
>
> (b) For purposes of this section, "desecrate" means deface, damage, or otherwise physically mistreat in a way that the actor knows will seriously offend one or more persons likely to observe or discover his action.[51]

This sounds as though the statute is punishing only expressive conduct ("knowingly . . . offend[ing]," which would be akin to insulting—analyzed as communicative in Chapter 5). But, notes the Court,

> [a] tired person might, for example, drag a flag through the mud, knowing that this conduct is likely to offend others, and yet have no thought of expressing any idea; neither the language nor the Texas courts' interpretations of the statute precludes the possibility that such a person would be prosecuted for flag desecration.[52]

For this reason, the Court in *Texas v. Johnson* invalidated the statute only "as applied" to Johnson's conduct (which was conceded by all to be expressive), instead of striking down the statute on its face. Just as the statute in *O'Brien* was not invalid merely because some *other* conduct it covered might be expressive, the Texas statute was not valid merely because some *other* conduct it covered might be nonexpressive.

But we still do not have conduct that is "necessarily expressive."

Perhaps the case of *Smith v. Goguen*[53] comes closest to filling that gap. The statute at issue provided:

> Whoever publicly mutilates, tramples upon, defaces or treats contemptuously the flag of the United States . . . whether such flag is public or private property . . . shall be punished by a fine of not less than ten nor more than one hundred dollars or by imprisonment for not more than one year, or both.[54]

Goguen had been arrested while wearing an American flag sewn to the seat of his blue jeans; the Court noted that he "was not charged with any act of physical desecration" but only with "publicly treat[ing] contemptuously the flag of the United States."[55] Although it is (as always) possible to describe Goguen's conduct in a way that makes it nonexpressive (e.g., "transporting an extra piece of cloth via his pants"), the statute can fairly be described as punishing conduct just because it is expressive. As Justice (then Judge) Scalia usefully put it in the lower court *CCNV* case,

> what might be termed the more generalized guarantee of freedom of expression makes the communicative nature of conduct an inadequate *basis* for singling out that conduct for proscription. A law *directed at* the communicative nature of conduct must, like a law directed at speech itself, be justified by the substantial showing of need that the First Amendment requires.[56]

The inherently expressive nature of "treating contemptuously" is evident even from the dictionary definition:

> *Contempt, disdain, scorn* imply strong feelings of disapproval combined with disgust or derision. *Contempt* is disapproval tinged with disgust for what seems mean, base, or worthless: *to feel contempt for a weakling.*[57]

And to violate the statute in this way, notes Justice White, "it is not enough that one 'treat' the flag; he must also treat it 'contemptuously,' which, in ordinary understanding, is the expression of contempt for the flag."[58] Indeed, it is hard to see how Goguen's treatment of the flag would even be covered by the statute if his conduct were not expressive. The difference between "treating contemptuously" (*Goguen*) and "seriously offending" (*Texas v. Johnson*) is that the latter focuses solely on the audience's reaction, leaving open the possibility that the "speaker" lacks the intent to communicate (as discussed in Chapter 5).

The foregoing analysis produces the following categorization:

Necessarily noncommunicative (*Kovacs v. Cooper*)
Possibly noncommunicative (*United States v. O'Brien*)
Possibly communicative (*Texas v. Johnson*)
Necessarily communicative (*Smith v. Goguen*)[59]

Again, though, "necessarily" is a relative term, referring not to limits on the description of expressive conduct (it can always be described as nonexpressive too) but to limits on the coverage of the relevant legislation.

In *Kovacs*, the ordinance's prohibition was limited to nonexpressive conduct (operating a "loud and raucous" sound truck), even though particular actions that might be covered by the ordinance (e.g., Kovacs's speech) could be described as expressive. It should be possible to ban *noise* without thereby running afoul of the Constitution's protection of *speech*, and the *Kovacs* Court seems satisfied that Trenton has done just that. In *O'Brien*, by contrast, there seemed to be a very real possibility that Congress was suppressing a particularly inflammatory form of protest when it banned the "knowing destruction or mutilation" of draft cards. Indeed, that seems to be the obvious interpretation, so perhaps the Court simply gave Congress the benefit of the doubt:

> While both [the Senate and House Armed Services Committee] reports make clear a concern with the "defiant" destruction of so-called "draft cards" and with "open" encouragement to others to destroy their cards, both reports also indicate that this concern stemmed from an apprehension that unrestrained destruction of cards would disrupt the smooth functioning of the Selective Service System.[60]

In *Texas v. Johnson*, the clear import of the statute was to ban conduct that normally would be described as expressive ("desecrating" the flag in a way that one knows will "seriously offend" others), but the very terms of the statute left open the possibility that the banned conduct could take place in a nonexpressive way (the tired person who simply drags a flag through the mud, with "no thought of expressing any idea"). The Court thus considered the statute only "as applied" to Johnson's conduct, which was concededly expressive. And, finally, in *Goguen* there was simply no way to interpret the statute's ban on "treating the flag contemptuously" as applying to anything other than expressive or communicative conduct.

V.

Reconsider now the objection: "Any action can be made communicative. Therefore it is impossible for courts to distinguish speech from other forms of intentional action." There is a great deal of truth to the first part, and much of what I have said above shows how actions can be made communicative. It was particularly easy to find speech at issue in *Spence v. Washington*, for example, because the defendant had taped one preexisting symbol (the peace symbol) onto another (the American flag). Flags, crosses, and other well-known symbols are, one might say, "inherently expressive." Practically anything one does to or with them means something, because they are *already expressive* in their own right in multiple historical contexts.

But, as suggested above, other things and actions can be made expressive too, if only we provide them with suitable contexts. Conduct that is not speech in the usual senses but is intended to communicate may, under the right circumstances, count as speech for First Amendment purposes. This applies even to things and actions that are not normally thought of as expressive or communicative at all. Driving too fast and breaking the speed limit, for example, are not normally thought of as expressive. But suppose a certain group takes issue with the speed limits and finds them too restrictive, inconsistent with natural law, or whatever. Suppose further that the group wants to publicize its grievances and draw attention to its concerns; so it organizes a "Day of Speeding," during which its members will deliberately break the speed limits at designated times and places.

Given this context and with enough public awareness, if you happened by on the "Day of Speeding" and saw a car rushing by at great speed, precisely at one of the designated times and places, you might very well think to yourself:

> There goes one of those speed limit protestors, trying to make a point.

(Here the speeder's intentional action would be communicative.) Let's assume that on any other day you would merely have thought:

> Wow! That car was really going fast—too fast.

(Here the speeder's intentional action would be noncommunicative.) So the speed limit protestors might very well succeed in communicating by speeding, given the unusual context they have created.

Does this mean that the speed limit protestors have a First Amendment defense to their violation of the law? That our speed limits are in danger of being struck down as unconstitutional? Or that courts would find it difficult here "to distinguish speech from other forms of intentional action"?

The short answer is "No," and the short reason is that not all conduct intended to communicate counts as *speech* for constitutional purposes; and not all that does is *protected* by the First Amendment.[61] So one should first ask, "Is it speech?" and then ask "Is it protected speech?" The speeding example is designed to be a case in which courts would and should find that the activity—in the special circumstances described above—counts as *speech* for constitutional purposes. But that is hardly the end of the inquiry. In the *Spence* case, the Court went on to inquire into the purposes behind Washington's statute criminalizing "improper use" of the flag. In particular, the Court wanted to see whether this was "a case of prosecution for the expression of an idea through activity" or one "in an environment over which the State by necessity must have certain supervisory powers unrelated to expression."[62]

Corresponding to these two possibilities are two very different descriptions of "what happened." In the speed limit example, someone familiar with the protest plans might say, "There goes someone protesting the speed limit." But an equally valid description would be, "There goes someone driving very fast" (or more precisely—if it could be measured—"There goes someone driving at 80 miles per hour"). This is presumably the sort of description that someone unfamiliar with the protest plans would give. And indeed this is presumably the more usual sort of description (unless speed limit protests are becoming epidemic, which on the above facts they are not). Most important, this latter sort of description presumably captures what the legislators who wrote the speed limit law were responding to. They wrote a law to solve the safety problem of driving very fast, or over 80 miles per hour, or something similar. Although facts could be invented such that the legislators *really* were trying to squelch speed limit protests, those are not the facts of this example. But they are the facts of the *Spence* case, where the Court found that "no . . . governmental interest unrelated to expression has been advanced or can be supported on this record," and struck down the "improper use" statute.[63]

So there should be nothing surprising or mysterious or paradoxical about the fact that almost anything can be made expressive or communicative; that courts can readily distinguish what does and does not count as *speech* for constitutional purposes; and that even an activity that concededly counts as speech may yet be restricted or even criminalized, so long as there is *also* a way to describe it that has nothing to do with speech. Neither description is inherently superior or more accurate or true; but regulation of the meaningful content of speech is presumptively invalid under the First Amendment,[64] so the law looks to that completely separate, alternative track where things are described most naturally in terms of "fast-moving cars" and the like. If this is truly the descriptive basis of the law, it will not be invalidated merely because some clever and creative soul can turn an otherwise nonexpressive activity into a forum for communication.

Were this not the case, our legal system would indeed be on shaky ground. But as it is, we can all now relax, secure in the knowledge that our speed limit laws will never be subject to constitutional invalidation!

Acknowledgments

This book arrived at its present form by a circuitous route. Parts of it derive from a dissertation on the philosophy of history.[1] Parts were inspired by a course in music theory I once taught.[2] Around the same time, I spent a summer at Stanford University studying medieval European epic (under the auspices of the National Endowment for the Humanities and Ted Andersson of the Department of German Studies) and wrote a paper of some relevance to the present study.[3] More recently, I spent another entire summer researching the decipherment of Linear B, only to conclude that this fascinating chapter in the history of ideas did not really fit in here.[4]

A more direct path to the present project can be traced through the following: "Hate Speech and the Mind-Body Problem: A Critique of Postmodern Censorship Theory," 7 *Legal Theory* 203 (2001); "Speech and Communication in Law and Philosophy," 12 *Legal Theory* 1 (2006).

In the face of unimaginable obstacles, unmentionable opposition, and uninterrupted interruptions, I am all the more grateful to have been the beneficiary of considerable assistance. I thank two anonymous reviewers for Oxford University Press and Larry Alexander, Edward Cleary,

Robert D'Amico, Lee Davidson, Dan Farber, Lyrissa Lidsky, Al Martinich, Tom Morawetz, Bill Page, Robert Post, Fred Schauer, Pieter Seuren, and Chris Slobogin for helpful comments, suggestions, and criticisms. Early versions of Chapters 1–3 were presented to the University of Florida Department of Philosophy, where John Biro, Robert D'Amico, Kirk Ludwig, and others helped rein in many wayward thoughts. My students in First Amendment Theory helped me more than they could realize.

For the support of my research in Germany, I am greatly indebted to the Alexander von Humboldt Stiftung; to my sponsors Ralf Dreier and Wolfgang Naucke; and to my colleagues Delf Buchwald, Klaus Lüderssen, Lorenz Schulz, and the late Walter Weyrauch. The University of Florida College of Law provided summer research appointments and a sabbatical leave.

Much of what I know of constitutional law came by way of Gerald Gunther. I imagine he is giving the departed Justices a rather lengthy lecture right about now. This book is dedicated to his memory.

Notes

Chapter 1: Meanings

1. PAUL GRICE, *Meaning*, *in* STUDIES IN THE WAY OF WORDS 213 (1989).
2. *Id.* at 214.
3. ROBERT M. MARTIN, THE MEANING OF LANGUAGE 223 (1987).
4. EUCLID, 1 THE ELEMENTS bk. 1, def. 15 (Thomas L. Heath trans., 2d revised ed. 1956).
5. KENNETH TAYLOR, TRUTH AND MEANING 311 (1998). Similarly, Grice distinguishes "timeless" meaning from occasion-meaning. *See* PAUL GRICE, *Utterer's Meaning, Sentence-Meaning, and Word-Meaning*, *in* STUDIES IN THE WAY OF WORDS, *supra*, at 117.
6. Adapted from Paul Ziff, *On H.P. Grice's Account of Meaning*, 28 ANALYSIS 1, 5 (1967); *see* MARTIN, *supra*, at 86, 90.
7. Ziff reports further that "[o]f course [the man] did not produce the effect he was after since no one recognized what his intention was."

   > Nonetheless that he had such an intention became clear. Being deemed mad, he was turned over to a psychiatrist. He complained to the psychiatrist that when he cried "Gleeg gleeg gleeg!" he had such an intention but no one recognized his intention and were they not mad not to do so.

   Ziff, *supra*.

8. A separate category of *utterance meaning* might be interposed between speaker's meaning and expression meaning. Expressions have a kind of objective, timeless status, but the utterance of an expression on a particular occasion is an act done by a particular speaker who presumably has some specific purpose in mind. "[I]n speaking one acts for a reason. Speaking is one of the ways in which we can effect change in the world, and in speaking we usually intend to make some change." Michael S. Moore, *The Semantics of Judging*, 54 S. CAL. L. REV. 151, 249 (1981); *cf. id.* at 246–56. The meaning of an utterance relates back to what the speaker meant in uttering it, which in turn reflects the speaker's underlying intentions in uttering it. Here, as Holmes put it, "we inquire what he meant in order to find out what he has said." Oliver Wendell Holmes, *The Theory of Legal Interpretation*, 12 HARV. L. REV. 417, 418 (1899); *see* Chapter 5, Part III *infra. See also* PIETER A.M. SEUREN, 1 LANGUAGE FROM WITHIN, LANGUAGE IN COGNITION 282–83 (2009):

> [I]t has become customary in linguistic semantics to use different terms for the meaning of sentence[s] and of utterances. . . . Since the middle of the twentieth century it has been normal practice, in circles of nonformal, structuralist, semanticists, to speak of *meaning* as a . . . property of sentences, and of *interpretation* as a . . . process involving utterances.

9. *See, e.g.*, STEPHEN R. SCHIFFER, MEANING (1972).
10. GRICE, *supra*, at 213.
11. *See* STEPHEN JAY GOULD, WONDERFUL LIFE: THE BURGESS SHALE AND THE NATURE OF HISTORY 60 (1989).
12. *Id.* at 116 (quoting H.B. Whittington).
13. *Id.* (emphasis added).
14. *See* HERMANN WEYL, SYMMETRY 25–38 (1952).
15. Bill Alpert, *Quants Live! The Revenge of the Big Brains*, BARRON'S, April 8, 2002, at T1.
16. In this connection there is also a sense of *mean* as "to be of importance."

> [T]he verb *mean* is frequently used, in common speech, to denote the all-important general phenomenon in human and animal life of having a degree of importance, as in *Only then did she realize what her family had meant to her.* Obviously, the phenomenon itself of something or somebody having importance for someone antedates human language by a long shot, but the

> use of the English word *mean* to refer to it is relatively recent. This use of *mean* is the result of normal processes of extension of lexical meaning, in this case of the word *mean*. . . .

SEUREN, *supra*, at 280; *cf.* OXFORD ENGLISH DICTIONARY ONLINE (2d ed. 1989) (Draft Revision Sept. 2008) (*mean*, v.):

> to be important to a person. . . . [1888] "It was only by a great effort that he could turn his thoughts from the Squire, and all that the Squire had meant to him during the past year."

17. These examples are drawn from SEUREN, *supra*, at 327–29.

18. *Id.* at 328–29.

19. MAURICE MERLEAU-PONTY, THE STRUCTURE OF BEHAVIOR 36 (Alden L. Fisher trans., 1963).

20. *Id.*

21. *Cf.* WILLIAM JAMES, 1 THE PRINCIPLES OF PSYCHOLOGY 402–04 (Dover ed. 1950) (1890):

> [S]uch writers as Locke, Hume, Hartley, the Mills, and Spencer . . . are bent on showing how the higher faculties of the mind are pure products of 'experience;' and experience is supposed to be of something simply *given*. . . . But the moment one thinks of the matter, one sees how false a notion of experience that is which would make it tantamount to the mere presence to the senses of an outward order. Millions of items of the outward order are present to my senses which never properly enter into my experience. Why? Because they have no interest for me. My experience is what I agree to attend to. Only those items which I notice shape my mind—without selective interest, experience is an utter chaos. Interest alone gives accent and emphasis, light and shade, background and foreground—intelligible perspective, in a word. . . .
>
> Everyone knows what attention is. It is the taking possession by the mind, in clear and vivid form, of one out of what seem several simultaneously possible objects or trains of thought. Focalization, concentration, of consciousness are of its essence. It implies withdrawal from some things in order to deal effectively with others. . . .

22. *See* ERIC R. KANDEL, IN SEARCH OF MEMORY: THE EMERGENCE OF A NEW SCIENCE OF MIND 296–97 (2006):

> The Gestalt psychologists argued that our coherent perceptions are the end result of the brain's built-in ability to derive meaning

from the properties of the world, only limited features of which can be detected by the peripheral sensory organs. The reason that the brain can derive meaning from, say, a limited analysis of a visual scene is that the visual system does not simply record a scene passively, as a camera does. Rather, perception is creative: the visual system transforms the two-dimensional patterns of light on the retina of the eye into a logically coherent and stable interpretation of a three-dimensional sensory world. Built into neural pathways of the brain are complex rules of guessing; those rules allow the brain to extract information from relatively impoverished patterns of incoming neural signals and turn it into a meaningful image. The brain is thus the ambiguity-resolving machine par excellence!

23. I am reminded of the Star Academy, "a place where every child is a star" (in other words, a place where there are no stars). One thinks also of Lake Wobegon, where "all the women are strong, all the men are good-looking, and all the children are above average." Garrison Keillor, *A Prairie Home Companion* (Minnesota Public Radio series).

24. Merleau-Ponty, *supra*, at 36.

25. For a description of more recent research, see Kandel, *supra*, at 300–02:

> In the early 1950s, Stephen Kuffler recorded from single cells in the retina and made the surprising discovery that those cells do not signal absolute levels of light; rather, they signal the contrast between light and dark. He found that the most effective stimulus for exciting retinal cells is not diffuse light but small spots of light. David Hubel and Torsten Wiesel found a similar principle operating in the next relay stage, located in the thalamus. However, they made the astonishing discovery that once the signal reaches the cortex, it is transformed. Most cells in the cortex do not respond vigorously to small spots of light. Instead, they respond to linear contours, to elongated edges between lighter and darker areas, such as those that delineate objects in our environment.
>
> Most amazingly, each cell in the primary visual cortex responds only to a specific orientation of such light-dark contours. Thus if a square block is rotated slowly before our eyes, slowly changing

the angle of each edge, different cells will fire in response to these different angles. Some cells respond best when the linear edge is oriented vertically, others when the edge is horizontal, and still other cells when the axis is at an oblique angle. Deconstructing visual objects into line segments of different orientation appears to be the initial step in encoding the forms of objects in our environment. . . .

. . .These scientists confirmed the inferences of the Gestalt psychologists by showing us that . . . [t]he brain does not simply take the raw data that it receives through the senses and reproduce it faithfully. Instead, each sensory system first analyzes and deconstructs, then restructures the raw, incoming information according to its own built-in connections and rules—shades of Immanuel Kant! . . . [A]s Mountcastle pointed out: . . . "*Sensation is an abstraction, not a replication, of the real world.*"

26. Daniel L. Schacter, The Seven Sins of Memory 9 (2001).

27. *Id.* at 164.

28. In one famous series of experiments, chess players of various skill levels were briefly shown positions from actual chess games and then asked to reconstruct them from memory. *See* William G. Chase & Herbert A. Simon, *Perception in Chess*, 4 Cognitive Psychol. 55 (1973); Adriaan D. de Groot, *Thought and Choice in Chess: An Overview of a Study Based on Selzean Theory, in* Otto Selz: His Contribution to Psychology 192 (Nico H. Frijda & Adriaan D. de Groot eds., 1982); A.D. de Groot, Thought and Choice in Chess (1965). The principal finding was that the ability to reconstruct the positions was directly proportional to chess skill: grandmasters could replace about 16 pieces correctly, while novices could replace only about 4.

Then, in a second phase of the experiment, the same subjects were shown the same pieces on the board—but arranged randomly, rather than in positions from actual games. Under these conditions, the chess masters did no better at replacing the pieces than the novices.

Here is a standard explanation for these results: "Thus, the ability exhibited by expert chess players represents a chess-specific skill that depends in large part on previous encounters with multiple patterns of chess pieces during years of playing actual chess games. This ability allows chess players to construct perceptual groupings of pieces and to remember these groupings." LARRY R. SQUIRE, MEMORY AND BRAIN 131 (1987). But consider those random positions: sometimes both kings were in check, both queens threatened, pawns poised to capture rooks, bishops on the same color squares, etc. *See, e.g., id.* at 132, Fig. 32. To the experts, these could hardly have been considered "chess" positions at all; they were, at best, meaningless arrangements of chess pieces—perhaps not unlike the work of small children. If memory is indeed structured in terms of meaningfulness, then it should be no surprise that the experts had so little to go on. By contrast, the actual chess positions (some taken from championship games) offered deep, rationally structured, multiple levels of meaning—for those who could grasp it.

29. DANIEL L. SCHACTER, SEARCHING FOR MEMORY 45–46 (1996).

30. Or see Elizabeth S. Parker, Larry Cahill & James L. McGaugh, *A Case of Unusual Autobiographical Remembering*, 12 NEUROCASE 35 (2006); JILL PRICE, THE WOMAN WHO CAN'T FORGET: THE EXTRAORDINARY STORY OF LIVING WITH THE MOST REMARKABLE MEMORY KNOWN TO SCIENCE—A MEMOIR (2008). Another fascinating case is reported in A.R. LURIA, THE MIND OF A MNEMONIST (1987) (1968).

31. SCHACTER, THE SEVEN SINS OF MEMORY, *supra*, at 190.

32. JORGE LUIS BORGES, *Funes, the Memorious, in* FICCIONES 112 (Anthony Kerrigan trans. 1962).

33. *Id.*

34. *Id.* at 112-13.

35. *Id.* at 114.

36. *Id.* at 115.

37. SCHACTER, SEARCHING FOR MEMORY, *supra*, at 81.

38. SCHACTER, THE SEVEN SINS OF MEMORY, *supra*, at 187.

39. SCHACTER, SEARCHING FOR MEMORY, *supra*, at 91.

40. *See generally* HEINRICH SCHENKER, FREE COMPOSITION (*Der freie Satz*) (Ernst Oster ed. & trans., 1979) (1935, 1956) (elaborating and distinguishing three levels of musical structure: background, middleground, and foreground).

41. VICTOR ZUCKERKANDL, THE SENSE OF MUSIC 11 (1971).

42. *Id.* at 12.

43. *Id.* at 19.

44. *Id.* at 30.

45. *See, e.g.*, WALTER PISTON, HARMONY 83–105 (Mark Devoto ed., 4th revised ed. 1978).

46. ZUCKERKANDL, *supra*, at 11.

47. *See* DAVID G. HUGHES, A HISTORY OF EUROPEAN MUSIC: THE ART MUSIC TRADITION OF WESTERN CULTURE 237–40 (1974); *cf. id.* at xiii:

> [W]e can identify an incomplete piece of music as easily as an incomplete work of literature. This results from a peculiar property of sounds (considering only musical ones for the moment), which, when properly used, fuse together into an interacting system wherein certain pitches become important in varying degrees, while others remain clearly subordinate. Thus even the first four or five notes of a melody interact to create in the listener a pattern of expectations, and the remainder of the tune consists of the fulfillment of these expectations, usually interspersed with intentional deceptions that heighten the tension and make the ultimate fulfillment that much more satisfying.

48. ZUCKERKANDL, *supra*, at 56.

49. *Id.* at 40; *cf.* HUGHES, *supra*, at xiii ("The tones of the melody have arranged themselves into a hierarchy that demands certain continuations and a certain conclusion, and prohibits others.").

50. HUGHES, *supra*, at xiii.

Chapter 2: Symbols

1. FERDINAND DE SAUSSURE, COURSE IN GENERAL LINGUISTICS 68 (Roy Harris trans., 1986); COURS DE LINGUISTIQUE GÉNÉRALE 101 (publié par Charles Bally et Albert Sechehaye avec la collaboration de Albert Riedlinger, édition critique préparée par Tullio de Mauro, Grande Bibliothèque Payot 1995) (1916) ("un rudiment de lien naturel").

2. ERNST CASSIRER, LANGUAGE AND MYTH 7 (Susanne K. Langer trans., 1953).

3. *See* DAVID HUME, AN INQUIRY CONCERNING HUMAN UNDERSTANDING § X (Charles W. Hendel ed., 1955) ("No testimony is sufficient to establish a miracle unless the testimony be of such a kind that its

falsehood would be more miraculous than the fact which it endeavors to establish.").

4. Karl R. Popper, Objective Knowledge 38–39 (Revised ed. 1979).
5. *Id.* at 39 n.7.
6. Immanuel Kant, Critique of Pure Reason, B xvii–xviii (my translation).
7. *Id.* at B xviii.
8. Ernst Cassirer, 1 The Philosophy of Symbolic Forms 76 (Ralph Manheim trans., 1955).
9. *Id.* at 102, 100.
10. *Id.* at 102.
11. Cassirer, Language and Myth, *supra*, at 32.
12. *See* Kant, *supra*, at A 111 ("The *a priori* conditions of a possible experience in general are at the same time conditions of the possibility of objects of experience.").
13. Cassirer, 1 The Philosophy of Symbolic Forms, *supra*, at 106.
14. *Id.* at 108.
15. *See* Ezra Pound, A B C of Reading 36 (New Directions ed. 1960) (1934):

> 'Great literature is simply language charged with meaning to the utmost possible degree.'
>
> Dichten = condensare.
>
> I begin with poetry because it is the most concentrated form of verbal expression. Basil Bunting, fumbling about with a German-Italian dictionary, found that this idea of poetry as concentration is as old almost as the German language. 'Dichten' is the German verb corresponding to the noun 'Dichtung' meaning poetry, and the lexicographer has rendered it by the Italian verb meaning 'to condense.'

There is a sense of *dichten* meaning "to make thick, tight, or impenetrable, esp. airtight or watertight" (from *dicht*, "thick, tight, dense") and another sense meaning "to devise, invent, express in writing, compose verses or poetry" (borrowed from Latin *dictare*, "to dictate something that is to be written down"). *See* Wahrig Deutsches Wörterbuch 913 (1975); Oxford English Dictionary Online (2d ed. 1989) (*dight*, v.); Hensleigh Wedgwood, A Dictionary of English Etymology 212 (2d ed. 1872) (glossing *dight*); Walter W. Skeat,

AN ETYMOLOGICAL DICTIONARY OF THE ENGLISH LANGUAGE 166 (2d ed. 1893) (glossing *dight*). Perhaps Pound may be viewed, at best, as suggesting a deeper underlying connection between the two senses. We can appreciate Pound's insight into the creative process without adopting his etymology.

16. ERNST CASSIRER, 3 THE PHILOSOPHY OF SYMBOLIC FORMS 116 (Ralph Manheim trans., 1957); 1 THE PHILOSOPHY OF SYMBOLIC FORMS, *supra*, at 110.
17. *See* CASSIRER, 3 THE PHILOSOPHY OF SYMBOLIC FORMS, *supra*, at 114.
18. CASSIRER, 1 THE PHILOSOPHY OF SYMBOLIC FORMS, *supra*, at 89.
19. MIRCEA ELIADE, THE MYTH OF THE ETERNAL RETURN 3–4, 34 (Willard R. Trask trans., 1965) (1949).
20. *Id.* at 9.
21. *See id.* at 30.
22. *Id.* at 32.
23. *Cf.* LUDWIG WITTGENSTEIN, TRACTATUS LOGICO-PHILOSOPHICUS ¶ 5.6 (D.F. Pears & B.F. McGuinness trans., 1963) ("*The limits of my language* mean the limits of my world.").
24. CLAUDE LÉVI-STRAUSS, THE SAVAGE MIND 37 (1966) (emphasis added).
25. *See id.* at 56.
26. *See id.* at 54–56.
27. *See* CLAUDE LÉVI-STRAUSS, TOTEMISM 78 (Rodney Needham trans., 1963).
28. *Id.*
29. LÉVI-STRAUSS, THE SAVAGE MIND, *supra*, at 59.
30. BRONISLAW MALINOWSKI, MAGIC, SCIENCE AND RELIGION 27 (1948).
31. Ursula McConnel, *The Wik-Munkan Tribe of Cape York Peninsula*, 1 OCEANIA 181, 183 (1930).
32. LÉVI-STRAUSS, TOTEMISM, *supra*, at 64.
33. *See, e.g.*, KARL POPPER, CONJECTURES AND REFUTATIONS ch. 1 (5th ed. 1989).
34. K.N. LLEWELLYN & E. ADAMSON HOEBEL, THE CHEYENNE WAY 3, 6–7, 9, 11–13, 30–31, 45 (1941).
35. JOHN STUART MILL, 1 A SYSTEM OF LOGIC, Book I, Chapter II, § 5 (9th ed. 1875) ("A man may have been named John, because that

was the name of his father; a town may have been named Dartmouth, because it is situated at the mouth of the Dart. But it is no part of the signification of the word John, that the father of the person so called bore the same name; nor even of the word Dartmouth, to be situated at the mouth of the Dart. If sand should choke up the mouth of the river, or an earthquake change its course, and remove it to a distance from the town, the name of the town would not necessarily be changed. That fact, therefore, can form no part of the signification of the word; for otherwise, when the fact confessedly ceased to be true, no one would any longer think of applying the name.").

36. *See* G. Cohen, *Why is it difficult to put names to faces?* 81 BRIT. J. PSYCH. 287 (1990); Carlo Semenza & Teresa Maria Sgaramella, *Production of Proper Names: A Clinical Case Study of the Effects of Phonemic Cueing*, 1 MEMORY 265 (1993).

37. DANIEL L. SCHACTER, THE SEVEN SINS OF MEMORY 63 (2001).

38. *See, e.g.*, Lochner v. New York, 198 U.S. 45, 70–71 (1905) (Harlan, J., dissenting):

> [I]n bakery and confectionery establishments . . . as all know, the air constantly breathed by workmen is not as pure and healthful as that to be found in some other establishments or out of doors.
>
> Professor Hirt in his treatise on the *Diseases of the Workers* has said: "The labor of the bakers is among the hardest and most laborious imaginable, because it has to be performed under conditions injurious to the health of those engaged in it. It is hard, very hard work, not only because it requires a great deal of physical exertion in an overheated workshop and during unreasonably long hours, but more so because of the erratic demands of the public, compelling the baker to perform the greater part of his work at night, thus depriving him of an opportunity to enjoy the necessary rest and sleep, a fact which is highly injurious to his health." Another writer says: "The constant inhaling of flour dust causes inflammation of the lungs and of the bronchial tubes. The eyes also suffer through this dust, which is responsible for the many cases of running eyes among the bakers. The long hours of toil to which all bakers are subjected produce rheumatism, cramps and swollen legs.

The intense heat in the workshops induces the workers to resort to cooling drinks, which together with their habit of exposing the greater part of their bodies to the change in the atmosphere, is another source of a number of diseases of various organs. Nearly all bakers are pale-faced and of more delicate health than the workers of other crafts, which is chiefly due to their hard work and their irregular and unnatural mode of living, whereby the power of resistance against disease is greatly diminished. The average age of a baker is below that of other workmen, they seldom live over their fiftieth year, most of them dying between the ages of forty and fifty."

Chapter 3: Signs

1. One might consult, for example, MICHEL FOUCAULT, LES MOTS ET LES CHOSES (1966); IAN HACKING, WHY DOES LANGUAGE MATTER TO PHILOSOPHY? (1975).
2. These examples are drawn from PIETER A.M. SEUREN, 1 LANGUAGE FROM WITHIN, LANGUAGE IN COGNITION 281 (2009).
3. *Id.* at 281–82.
4. This inference is discussed more fully in Chapter 5, Part III *infra*.
5. WAHRIG DEUTSCHES WÖRTERBUCH 3681 (1975). (This and the following two quotations are my translations.)
6. *Id.* at 2318.
7. *Id.* at 2720.
8. *Cf.* SEUREN, *supra*, at 293:

   > [A]ny language used for the description of meanings will again contain expressions that have a meaning, which will then again have to be described in terms of some language containing expressions that have a meaning, and so on *ad infinitum*. When ordinary language is used for the specification of lexical meanings, one will be forever caught up in a circle of synonymy.

   See also W.V. Quine, *Two Dogmas of Empiricism*, 60 PHIL. REV. 20, 24–31 (1951). Some of Quine's most important claims about definitions and synonyms are reevaluated in Paul Artin Boghossian, *Analyticity*, *in* A COMPANION TO THE PHILOSOPHY OF LANGUAGE 331 (Bob Hale & Crispin Wright eds., 1997).

9. Samuel Johnson, 1 A Dictionary of the English Language, Preface (2d ed. 1755); *cf.* subtitle: "In which the words are deduced from their originals, and illustrated in their different significations by examples from the best writers."

10. Simon Winchester, The Meaning of Everything: The Story of the Oxford English Dictionary 35–36 (2003).

11. Charles Richardson, 1 A New Dictionary of the English Language 538 (1837).

12. Richard Chenevix Trench, On Some Deficiencies in Our English Dictionaries 57 (1857).

13. 1 The Oxford English Dictionary, at xli (2d ed. 1989) (directions issued to readers in 1879).

14. *Cf.* J.L. Austin, *The Meaning of a Word*, *in* Philosophical Papers 55, 56 (J.O. Urmson & G.J. Warnock eds., 2d ed. 1970):

> [T]o say a word or a phrase 'has a meaning' is to say that there are sentences in which it occurs which 'have meanings': and to know the meaning which the word or phrase has, is to know the meanings of sentences in which it occurs. All the dictionary can do when we 'look up the meaning of a word' is to suggest aids to the understanding of sentences in which it occurs.

15. Ferdinand de Saussure, Course in General Linguistics 68 (Roy Harris trans., 1986) [hereinafter Course]; 1 Cours de linguistique générale 155 (édition critique par Rudolf Engler, Otto Harrassowitz 1989) (1916) [hereinafter Cours].

16. "[L]anguage characterized by circumlocution and jargon, usually hard to understand: *the gobbledegook of government reports*." The Random House Dictionary of the English Language 817 (2d unabridged ed. 1987).

17. *Id.* at 906.

18. *See* Edmund Leach, Culture and Communication 21, 48 (1976); John Lyons, 1 Semantics 66 (1977).

19. Leach, *supra*, at 47.

20. Claude Lévi-Strauss, Structural Anthropology 61 (Claire Jacobson & Brooke Grundfest Schoepf trans,. 1963).

21. *See id.* at 93.

22. *See* Lyons, *supra*, at 70–71.

23. Ernst Cassirer, An Essay on Man 115 (1944).

24. *See id.* at 115–18.
25. LYONS, *supra*, at 100.
26. SAUSSURE, COURSE at 68–69; COURS at 155.
27. COURSE at 68; COURS at 155.
28. COURSE at 73; COURS at 162.
29. *Id.*
30. *See* Law No. 94-665 of 4 August 1994 Relative to the Use of the French Language. Examples drawn from canine cuisine would include *languettes à croquer de cuir brut* for "rawhide munchy strips" and *os de cuir brut de taille petite* for "small rawhide bones."
31. LÉVI-STRAUSS, STRUCTURAL ANTHROPOLOGY, *supra*, at 90.
32. *See id.*
33. *Id.*
34. *Id.* at 90–91.
35. *Id.* at 91.
36. *See* SAUSSURE, COURSE at 130–32; COURS at 297–303.
37. COURSE at 131; COURS at 301.
38. *Id.*
39. Émile Benveniste, *La forme et le sens dans le langage*, *in* LE LANGAGE II: ACTES DU XIIIe CONGRÈS DES SOCIÉTÉS DE PHILOSOPHIE DE LANGUE FRANÇAISE 29, 35 (Neuchâtel, 1967), *reprinted in* 2 PROBLÈMES DE LINGUISTIQUE GÉNÉRALE 215, 223 (1974) ("To be distinctive, to be significant—it's the same thing."); *cf.* ÉTIENNE GILSON, LINGUISTIQUE ET PHILOSOPHIE 263–83 (1969).
40. SAUSSURE, COURSE at 117 (emphasis added); COURS at 268 ("dans la limite où les sons restent distincts les uns des autres").
41. WAHRIG DEUTSCHES WÖRTERBUCH 4319 (1975); *cf.* DUDEN-OXFORD GROSSWÖRTERBUCH ENGLISCH 1649 (1990). I can personally attest that *zwo* is used in other contexts where understandability is at issue—particularly in German pubs, for example. (In truth, there is no such thing as a German pub, or café; but that is another story. *See* Part V *infra*.)
42. SAUSSURE, COURSE at 86; COURS at 192.
43. LYONS, *supra*, at 86–87.
44. *See generally* DONALD DAVIDSON, *Radical Interpretation*, *in* INQUIRIES INTO TRUTH AND INTERPRETATION 125 (1984); *On the Very Idea of a Conceptual Scheme*, *id.* at 183.

45. SAUSSURE, COURSE at 111; COURS at 253.

46. *Id.*

47. *See* COURSE at 107; COURS at 246.

48. *See generally* WILLIAM EMPSON, SEVEN TYPES OF AMBIGUITY (2d revised ed. 1947) (much great poetry depends on alternative, even contrary, meanings for "the same piece of language").

49. Once, during a tennis match on German television, the players seemed to be exclaiming that they had *missed* various shots. (Actually, they were saying German *Mist* ["dung"].) And once, while I was waiting in line at a German bank, the fellow next to me seemed strangely amused as I hurriedly wrote out a check for "sex hundert" marks.

But these are not the best examples, since English *mist* is actually related to *Mist*, and English *sex* does not really sound much like German *sechs* ("six"). (Maybe I was thinking of German *sex*, a homonym of *sechs*.)

50. *See* RANDOM HOUSE DICTIONARY OF THE ENGLISH LANGUAGE, *supra*, at 1706.

51. *See* LYONS, *supra*, at 237–38. But Lyons then cautions that the problem of incongruent boundaries between word meanings in different languages should not be overemphasized:

> Two languages might well differ with respect to the boundaries that they draw in a denotational continuum and yet be in agreement with respect to what is central, or focal, in the denotation of roughly equivalent words. . . . [S]tructuralists have overemphasized the importance of determining the denotational boundaries of words.

Id. at 247.

52. *See id.* at 235–38.

53. *Cf.* DONALD DAVIDSON, *Truth and Meaning*, *in* INQUIRIES INTO TRUTH AND INTERPRETATION 17, 24, 25 (1984):

> [G]iving necessary and sufficient conditions for the truth of every sentence . . . is a way of giving the meaning of a sentence. . . .
>
> . . . The theory reveals nothing new about the conditions under which an individual sentence is true; it does not make those conditions any clearer than the sentence itself does. The work of the theory is in relating the known truth conditions of

each sentence to those aspects ('words') of the sentence that recur in other sentences, and can be assigned identical roles in other sentences.

54. Claude Lévi-Strauss, Anthropologie structurale 107 (1962) (a word's meaning "depends on the way in which each language slices up the realm of signification to which the word belongs"); *cf.* Davidson, *Truth and Meaning*, *supra*, at 18, 22:

> [A] satisfactory theory of the meanings of complex expressions may not require entities as meanings of all the parts. It behoves us then to rephrase our demand on a satisfactory theory of meaning so as not to suggest that individual words must have meanings at all, in any sense that transcends the fact that they have a systematic effect on the meanings of the sentences in which they occur. . . .
>
> . . . [One should] not . . . assume that parts of sentences have meanings except in the ontologically neutral sense of making a systematic contribution to the meaning of the sentences in which they occur.

Chapter 4: Boundaries

1. Special issues arising in cases of statutory interpretation might seem to make expression meaning the primary focus there; but for a problem of statutory interpretation to arise, speaker's meaning would already have had to be conveyed. *See, e.g.*, Oliver Wendell Holmes, *The Theory of Legal Interpretation*, 12 Harv. L. Rev. 417, 418–20 (1899); Reed Dickerson, The Interpretation and Application of Statutes 34–38 (1975).

   Chapter 3, Part I analyzed sentence meaning as the primary repository of linguistic meaning, but the emphasis there was on sentence meaning *as opposed to* word meaning. *See also* Chapter 5, Parts II–III *infra.*

2. Ferdinand de Saussure, Course in General Linguistics 71, 72 (Roy Harris trans., 1986) (1916).

3. *Cf.* David Wiggins, *Meaning and Truth Conditions: From Frege's Grand Design to Davidson's, in* A Companion to the Philosophy of Language 3, 20 (Bob Hale & Crispin Wright eds., 1997) ("Generally speaking, what makes interpretation possible is the fact that the

language to which the sentences belong can be treated as *pre-existing* any particular speaker or hearer and any particular act of communication. It is something that speakers and hearers need to know about already.").

4. *Cf.* DONALD DAVIDSON, *Truth and Meaning*, *in* INQUIRIES INTO TRUTH AND INTERPRETATION 17 (1984). Davidson says the line he is taking points to "a certain holistic view of meaning":

   > If sentences depend for their meaning on their structure, and we understand the meaning of each item in the structure only as an abstraction from the totality of sentences in which it features, then we can give the meaning of any sentence (or word) only by giving the meaning of every sentence (and word) in the language. Frege said that only in the context of a sentence does a word have meaning; in the same vein he might have added that only in the context of the language does a sentence (and therefore a word) have meaning.

   Id. at 22.

5. THE RANDOM HOUSE DICTIONARY OF THE ENGLISH LANGUAGE 1063 (2d unabridged ed. 1987).
6. Sergeant David Karsnia, Arrest Report, Metropolitan Airports Commission Police Department, Hennepin County, Minnesota (June 12, 2007).
7. *See generally* Laura M. Mac Donald, *America's Toe-Tapping Menace*, N.Y. TIMES, Sept. 2, 2007, § 4 (Week in Review), at 10.
8. Brief of Amici Curiae American Civil Liberties Union et al., at 5–6, Minnesota v. Craig, Hennepin County District Court (No. 27-CR-07-043231).
9. Minnesota v. Craig, No. 27-CR-07-043231, Order and Memorandum at 26 (Hennepin County District Court, October 4, 2007).
10. U.S. CONST. amend. I.
11. WILLIAM BLACKSTONE, 4 COMMENTARIES *151–52; *cf.* JOSEPH STORY, 3 COMMENTARIES ON THE CONSTITUTION OF THE UNITED STATES § 1879 (1833) ("the liberty of the press, as understood by all England, is the right to publish without any previous restraint, or license"); *id.* § 1874:

   > That [the First] amendment was intended to secure to every citizen an absolute right to speak, or write, or print, whatever

> he might please, without any responsibility, public or private, therefor, is a supposition too wild to be indulged by any rational man. . . . It is plain, then, that the language of this amendment imports no more, than that every man shall have a right to speak, write, and print his opinions upon any subject whatsoever, without any prior restraint, so always, that he does not injure any other person in his rights, person, property, or reputation; and so always, that he does not thereby disturb the public peace, or attempt to subvert the government.

See also JAMES KENT, 2 COMMENTARIES ON AMERICAN LAW 23 (2d ed. 1832):

> [T]he current of opinion seems to have been setting strongly, not only in favour of erecting barriers against any previous restraints upon publications, (and which was all that the earlier sages of the revolution had in view,) but in favour of the policy that would diminish or destroy altogether every obstacle or responsibility in the way of the publication of the truth.

12. Patterson v. Colorado, 205 U.S. 454, 462 (1907).
13. Schenck v. United States, 249 U.S. 47, 51–52 (1919).
14. Near v. Minnesota, 283 U.S. 697, 714–15 (1931); *cf.* Grosjean v. American Press Co., 297 U.S. 233, 246 (1936) ("mere exemption from previous censorship was soon recognized as too narrow a view of the liberty of the press").
15. THOMAS M. COOLEY, CONSTITUTIONAL LIMITATIONS 604 (7th ed. 1903).
16. 315 U.S. 568, 571–72 (1942). The Court went on to add that "[r]esort to epithets or personal abuse is not in any proper sense communication of information or opinion safeguarded by the Constitution, and its punishment as a criminal act would raise no question under that instrument" (quoting Cantwell v. Connecticut, 310 U.S. 296, 309–10 (1940)).
17. HARRY KALVEN, JR., A WORTHY TRADITION 18 (Jamie Kalven ed., 1988) (emphasis added).
18. *See* DAVID M. RABBAN, FREE SPEECH IN ITS FORGOTTEN YEARS 27–44 (1997).
19. *Ex parte* Jackson, 96 U.S. 727, 735–36 (1878).
20. 354 U.S. 476 (1957).

21. *Id.* at 481, 484–86 (quoting Beauharnais v. Illinois, 343 U.S. 250, 266 (1952)).

22. *See* HARRY KALVEN, JR., *supra*, at 36–37.

23. *Roth*, 354 U.S. at 514 (Douglas, J., dissenting); *cf.* Harry Kalven, Jr., *The Metaphysics of the Law of Obscenity*, 1960 SUP. CT. REV. 1, 10–11:

> The two-level speech theory, although it afforded the Court a statesmanlike way around a dilemma, seems difficult to accept as doctrine. It is perhaps understandable in the context of *Chaplinsky*, where the speech in question is nothing more complex than the utterance "son of a bitch," said rapidly. In connection with libel, as in *Beauharnais*, or obscenity, as in *Roth*, however, it seems a strained effort to trap a problem. At one level there are communications which, even though odious to the majority opinion of the day, even though expressive of the thought we hate, are entitled to be measured against the clear-and-present-danger criterion. At another level are communications apparently so worthless as not to require any extensive judicial effort to determine whether they can be prohibited. There is to be freedom for the thought we hate, but not for the candor we deplore.

24. Stanley v. Georgia, 394 U.S. 557, 565 (1969).

25. *Id.* at 559; *see also id.* at 563:

> *Roth* and its progeny certainly do mean that the First and Fourteenth Amendments recognize a valid governmental interest in dealing with the problem of obscenity. But the assertion of that interest cannot, in every context, be insulated from all constitutional protections. Neither *Roth* nor any other decision of this Court reaches that far.

26. HARRY KALVEN, JR., A WORTHY TRADITION, *supra*, at 19; *cf. id.* at 17–19, 48–59.

27. *See* Cohen v. California, 403 U.S. 15, 18–20 (1971), discussed in Part IV *infra*.

28. Miller v. California, 413 U.S. 15, 21, 23 (1973).

29. *Id.* at 23.

30. *Id.* at 23–24.

31. *Id.* at 24 (emphasis added).

32. *Id.* at 25.

33. *See, e.g.*, Paris Adult Theatre I v. Slaton, 413 U.S. 49, 63 (1973) ("The sum of experience, including that of the past two decades, affords an ample basis for legislatures to conclude that a sensitive, key relationship of human existence . . . can be debased and distorted by crass commercial exploitation of sex.").

34. *See, e.g., id.* at 60–61 ("Although there is no conclusive proof of a connection between antisocial behavior and obscene material, the legislature of Georgia could quite reasonably determine that such a connection does or might exist.").

35. *See, e.g., id.* at 64 ("Nor do modern societies leave disposal of garbage and sewage up to the individual 'free will,' but impose regulation to protect both public health and the appearance of public places.").

36. *Id.* at 59 (quoting Alexander Bickel, 22 PUB. INT. 25–26 (Winter 1971) (emphasis added by the Court)).

37. 283 U.S. 697, 715 (1931); *see also* Robertson v. Baldwin, 165 U.S. 275, 281 (1897) ("the freedom of speech and of the press . . . does not permit the publication of libels, blasphemous or indecent articles, or other publications injurious to public morals or private reputation").

38. Beauharnais v. Illinois, 343 U.S. 250, 298 (1952) (Jackson, J., dissenting).

39. *Id.* at 251–53.

40. *Id.* at 255–57, 258, 263.

41. *Id.* at 266.

42. 376 U.S. 254, 270 (1964).

43. *Id.* at 269.

44. *Id.* at 279 (emphasis added).

45. *See* Philadelphia Newspapers, Inc. v. Hepps, 475 U.S. 767 (1986); Milkovich v. Lorain Journal Co., 497 U.S. 1, 19–20 (1990) (statements must be "provable as false" or contain "a provably false factual connotation" before there can be liability in defamation).

46. *See* Collin v. Smith, 578 F.2d 1197, 1204–05 (7th Cir. 1978) (expressing "doubt . . . that *Beauharnais* remains good law at all after the constitutional libel cases").

47. 343 U.S. at 272 (Black, J., dissenting).

48. *Id.* at 252.

49. *Id.* at 262.

50. *Id.* at 263.

51. *Milkovich*, 497 U.S. at 20.

52. *Id.* at 18.

53. *See* JAMES BERNOULLI, THE ART OF CONJECTURING, Part Four (Dep't of Statistics, Harvard U., Technical Report No. 2, Bing Sung trans., 1966) (1713). Putting it the other way around, "the probability that a sample mean will diverge from the population (true) mean tends toward zero as the size of the sample increases." ENCYCLOPÆDIA BRITANNICA, VI MICROPÆDIA 49 (15th ed. 1984).

54. CHARLES M. GRINSTEAD & J. LAURIE SNELL, INTRODUCTION TO PROBABILITY 305 (2d rev. ed. 1997).

55. *See, e.g.*, SAM KASH KACHIGAN, STATISTICAL ANALYSIS 110 (1986) ("[A]s the sample size increases it will become more and more improbable to get a sample composed preponderantly of extreme values resulting in an extreme sample mean.").

For example, with one random throw of a fair, six-sided die, the probability of getting the extreme low value of 1 is 1/6 or 16.7%. But with just one additional throw, the probability of getting the (combined) extreme low value of 2 drops to just 1/36 or 2.8%. For five throws, the corresponding probability is only .01%.

56. *Beauharnais*, 343 U.S. at 272 (Black, J., dissenting); *see* PROSSER AND KEETON, THE LAW OF TORTS § 111 (5th ed. 1984):

> Ordinarily, no action lies for the publication of a general condemnation concerning a large group or class of persons, simply because such a general condemnation could not reasonably be regarded as referring to each individual or any particular individual within the group; nor is it calculated to induce the reasonable belief of enough likelihood of its applicability to a particular person to impair or injure such person's reputation.

See also RESTATEMENT (SECOND) OF TORTS § 564A (1977) (liability in defamation to individual member only where group or class is so small that the statement can reasonably be understood to refer to that individual); Neiman-Marcus v. Lait, 13 F.R.D. 311 (S.D.N.Y. 1952) (no cause of action where the allegedly defamed group or class consisted of 382 saleswomen).

57. 315 U.S. at 572.

58. *Id.* at 573.

59. *Id.*

60. *Id.* at 572.

61. *Beauharnais*, 343 U.S. at 254.

62. *Id.* at 252.

63. PROSSER AND KEETON, *supra*.

64. *Beauharnais*, 343 U.S. at 273 (Black, J., dissenting).

65. Frederick Schauer, *The Boundaries of the First Amendment: A Preliminary Exploration of Constitutional Salience*, 117 HARV. L. REV. 1765, 1766 (2004).

66. *Id.* at 1767.

67. *Id.* at 1771, 1773.

68. 315 U.S. at 572 (quoting Cantwell v. Connecticut, 310 U.S. 296, 310 (1940)).

69. R.A.V. v. City of St. Paul, 505 U.S. 377, 383–85 (1992). The Court added that "[w]e have not said that [fighting words] constitute '*no* part of the expression of ideas,' but only that they constitute 'no *essential* part of any exposition of ideas.'" *Id.*

70. *See* JOHN HART ELY, DEMOCRACY AND DISTRUST 105–16 (1980).

71. Cohen v. California, 403 U.S. 15, 19–20, 24 (1971).

72. *See, e.g., R.A.V.*, 505 U.S. at 382 ("Content-based regulations are presumptively invalid.").

73. Schauer, *supra*, at 1773.

74. *Id.* at 1768.

75. Frohwerk v. United States, 249 U.S. 204, 206 (1919); *see also* Abrams v. United States, 250 U.S. 616, 627 (1919) (Holmes, J., dissenting).

76. Gompers v. Bucks Stove & Range Co., 221 U.S. 418, 439 (1911), *cited in Schenck*, 249 U.S. at 52.

77. Schauer, *supra*, at 1801–02; *cf.* Kent Greenawalt, *Speech and Crime*, 1980 AM. B. FOUND. RES. J. 675–80, 742–56.

78. Schauer, *supra*, at 1768.

Chapter 5: Intentions

1. Susan J. Brison, *Speech and Other Acts: A Reply to Charles W. Collier, "Hate Speech and the Mind-Body Problem: A Critique of Postmodern Censorship Theory,"* 10 LEGAL THEORY 261 (2004); *see also* Charles W. Collier, *Hate Speech and the Mind-Body Problem: A Critique of Postmodern Censorship Theory*, 7 LEGAL THEORY 203 (2001); Charles W. Collier, *Speech and Communication in Law and Philosophy*, 12 LEGAL THEORY 1 (2006).
2. Susan J. Brison, *Speech, Harm, and the Mind-Body Problem in First Amendment Jurisprudence*, 4 LEGAL THEORY 39, 61 (1998).
3. G.E.M. ANSCOMBE, INTENTION § 2, at 5 (2d ed. 1963).
4. Clark v. Community for Creative Non-Violence, 468 U.S. 288, 293 n.5 (1984); *see also* United States v. O'Brien, 391 U.S. 367, 376 (1968) ("We cannot accept the view that an apparently limitless variety of conduct can be labeled 'speech' whenever the person engaging in the conduct intends thereby to express an idea."); Miller v. Civil City of South Bend, 904 F.2d 1081, 1124 (7th Cir. 1990) (Easterbrook, J., dissenting):

   > "Speech" cannot be synonymous with purposive conduct, else the First Amendment means that "Congress shall make no law . . . abridging the freedom of conduct"—or, for short, "Congress shall make no law."

5. Spence v. Washington, 418 U.S. 405, 409–11 (1974).
6. Miller v. Civil City of South Bend, 904 F.2d 1081, 1092 (7th Cir. 1990) (Posner, J., concurring).
7. Brison, *Speech and Other Acts*, *supra*, at 263; *see also* Robert Post, *Recuperating First Amendment Doctrine*, 47 STAN. L. REV. 1249, 1250–52 (1995).
8. *See, e.g.*, DONALD DAVIDSON, *Psychology as Philosophy*, *in* ESSAYS ON ACTIONS AND EVENTS 229 (1980) ("an event is an action if and only if it can be described in a way that makes it intentional").
9. CARLOS J. MOYA, THE PHILOSOPHY OF ACTION 54 (1990).
10. Brison, *Speech and Other Acts*, *supra*, at 265.
11. *Id.*
12. *Id.*
13. Take, for example, the common form of greeting someone by raising your hand, and suppose that just as you are raising your hand to

scratch your head, a friend comes into view. If your friend thinks she has been greeted, does that mean you greeted her? If so, then it would never make sense to say that she *mistakenly* thought she had been greeted. And you should henceforth be *very* careful about raising your hand. . . .

14. Brison, *Speech and Other Acts*, *supra*, at 265.

15. 20 OXFORD ENGLISH DICTIONARY 703 (2d ed. 1989).

16. This is a case where philosophical usage diverges from legal usage (assuming one could make a legal case out of yawning). If a man replenishes a house's water supply with poisoned water, knowing full well it will poison the inhabitants but doing so only to earn his pay for supplying water, "it would be incorrect" (from a philosophical point of view) "to say that his act of replenishing the house supply with poisoned water was intentional." ANSCOMBE, *supra*, § 25, at 42. But that would hardly be a winning legal defense.

    Justice Brennan suggests a closer case: "A tired person might, for example, drag a flag through the mud, knowing that this conduct is likely to offend others, and yet have no thought of expressing any idea." Texas v. Johnson, 491 U.S. 397, 403 n.3 (1989). Even within philosophy there are objective, verifiable limits on what can credibly be claimed as one's intentions (unlike, say, dreams, which can be as incredible as you please). In Anscombe's example above, the analysis could go either way as details are filled in. If the provider of the poisoned water was in fact simply doing his usual job, following his normal routine, and, we might say, delivering the water "in spite of"—rather than "because of"—its being poisoned, that would be a very different case from one in which he was taking unusual measures and actively going out of his way to avoid detection. *See* ANSCOMBE, *supra*, §§ 23–25. One cannot simply make up a set of facts and stipulate, however implausibly, that the action in question is unintentional (at least if one wishes to convince anyone else).

    In other words, our intentions are not some sort of mental facts that we alone can truly *know*. Instead, intentions are revealed in what we would or could (plausibly) *say* in response to the question "Why?" ("Why did you do that?").

17. This and the following example are suggested by Peter Meijes Tiersma, *Nonverbal Communication and the Freedom of "Speech,"* 1993 WIS. L. REV. 1525, 1554, 1562.

18. *Cf.* PAUL GRICE, *Meaning*, *in* STUDIES IN THE WAY OF WORDS 213, 218 (1989):

> What we want to find is the difference between, for example, "deliberately and openly letting someone know" and "telling" and between "getting someone to think" and "telling."

19. Brison, *Speech and Other Acts, supra*, at 266.
20. Virginia v. Black, 538 U.S. 343, 352, 353–54, 357 (2003).
21. Brison, *Speech and Other Acts, supra*, at 266.
22. *Id.* at 265, 266. This example is not entirely hypothetical. *See* Virginia v. Black, 538 U.S. 343 (2003) (upholding convictions under statute making it unlawful "to burn, or cause to be burned, a cross . . . with the intent of intimidating any person").
23. Brison, *Speech and Other Acts, supra*, at 266.
24. *Id.* These quotations are taken from Brison's discussion of her own cross-burning example. If she objects that my new facts make the example noncommunicative, then we agree.
25. *Id.*
26. This example is suggested by MOYA, *supra*, at 38–39, 49–53.
27. Al Martinich writes:

> I can imagine being "greeted" by a robot in a Las Vegas casino. If the robot is sophisticated enough, the scare quotes may come off the word "greet."

I am at somewhat of a disadvantage here, having never been to Las Vegas. But on my facts, as reasonably interpreted, the "greeter" is known to be a machine or robot. So this is not the Turing Test (figuring out whether one's interlocutor is a human or a sophisticated computer program). *See, e.g.*, A.M. Turing, *Computing Machinery and Intelligence*, 59 MIND 433 (1950); ANDREW HODGES, ALAN TURING: THE ENIGMA 265–66, 414–21 (1983).

So, knowing that the "greeter" is a robot, I know that it is simply programmed to display all the outward signs of greeting. It cannot really know me or be in a position to make any commitment to me.

But if this truly were a case for the Turing Test, Martinich suggests how this analysis might have to be modified:

> I intended it to be a very sophisticated robot, one that can converse and interact with people. If a customer asks it where the blackjack tables are, it can tell her. If a customer holding out a

piece of paper asks the robot to give a message to the manager, it will reach out its arm, take the paper and give it to the manager. And so on. It seems to me to be merely a matter of time before machines this intelligent are developed. . . . It is arguable that there will come a time when some machines are so sophisticated that it will make sense to say that they can speak a language and have intentions.

E-mail correspondence (09/22/08, 10/08/08).

28. A clever reader might think to combine these two examples. Suppose you and I have arranged things so that when you return from summer vacation, I will "greet" you by kicking a ball through the goalposts. (Perhaps your house faces the goalposts, and the ball's passing through them would make for a dramatic welcome.) This would be communicative as well as meaningful, and here the communication indeed seems to depend upon an event in the physical world.

But suppose that on the appointed day, I kick the ball, and it narrowly fails to pass through the goalposts. I think it would be hard for us to maintain the fiction that I failed to communicate, because my intention to do so was so clearly evident (which, of course, would *not* be a good argument in the sports context—where we don't care about communication—when I narrowly miss the goalposts during a game).

Likewise, at an auction, people who cannot bid in the usual way (perhaps because of some physical disability) can still bid if their intention to do so is made sufficiently clear. *See* Collier, *Hate Speech and the Mind-Body Problem*, *supra*, at 211–12. When communication is at issue, there is almost nothing of a physical nature that cannot be dispensed with.

29. This analysis might have to be modified where linguistic or other higher-order conventional systems of meaning come into play. What about, for example, "accidentally" signaling for a left turn with the turn indicator while driving, or (less plausibly) "accidentally" insulting someone with a particular set of words while giving a speech? These could be analyzed as cases of "miscommunication" (gross miscommunication) since *some* communication was intended, but here the intentions themselves may be confused or questionable ("What were you *thinking* when you signaled for a left turn?"), rather than the actions taken to implement them.

30. If someone tells me you "offended Linda," and I ask you "Why?," you might very well respond, "I had no idea I was offending her"

or "I didn't mean to"—suggesting it was unintentional. But if it would, in principle, never make sense for me to ask "Why?" (if that would be like asking, "Why did you offend Linda with your snoring while you were asleep?"), then offending would not be your action, since it would not be intentional under any description; it would simply be an event.

31. 10 OXFORD ENGLISH DICTIONARY 725 (2d ed. 1989); 7 *id.* at 1057.

32. *See, e.g.*, Jennifer Steinhauer, *Schwarzenegger Apologizes for Ethnic Group Remarks*, N.Y. TIMES, Sept. 9, 2006, at A9:

> Mr. Schwarzenegger called a news conference in Los Angeles with Ms. Garcia at his side to make the standard political apology. "To anyone out there that feels offended by those comments, I just want to say I apologize," he said.

For a more sophisticated version, see Amy Chozick, *Hillary Clinton Says She Regrets Her Husband's Charged Comments*, WALL ST. J., Feb. 25, 2008, at A4:

> "If anyone was offended by anything that was said, whether it was meant or not, or misinterpreted or not, then obviously, I regret that," Mrs. Clinton said.

For an interesting analysis of the *faux pas*, see Martin P. Golding, *Faux Pas*, *in* PHILOSOPHIA PRACTICA UNIVERSALIS: FESTSCHRIFT FÜR JOACHIM HRUSCHKA (B. Sharon Byrd & Jan C. Joerden eds.), 13 JAHRBUCH FÜR RECHT UND ETHIK 103 (2005); *see generally* CAROL TAVRIS & ELLIOT ARONSON, MISTAKES WERE MADE (2007). For a comprehensive review, see Henry Alford, *Regrets Only*, N.Y. TIMES, Oct. 14, 2007 (Week in Review), at WK12.

33. *See generally* Larry Alexander, *Harm, Offense, and Morality*, 7 CANADIAN J.L. & JURISPRUDENCE 199 (1994); JOEL FEINBERG, 2 THE MORAL LIMITS OF THE CRIMINAL LAW: OFFENSE TO OTHERS (1985).

34. Brison, *Speech and Other Acts, supra,* at 265.

35. *See generally* LEONARD W. LEVY, BLASPHEMY (1993) (discussing serious offenders from Socrates to Salman Rushdie).

36. O.W. HOLMES, JR., THE COMMON LAW 3 (1881); *cf.* WILLIAM SHAKESPEARE, A MIDSUMMER NIGHT'S DREAM act 3, sc. 2:

> You are unkind, Demetrius; be not so;
>
> For you love Hermia; this you know I know.

37. Kurt Gray & Daniel M. Wegner, *The Sting of Intentional Pain*, 19 PSYCHOL. SCI. 1260 (2008) ("In a sense, intended harms are events

initiated by one mind to communicate meaning (malice) to another, and this could shape the recipient's experience. . . . In an interpersonal context, the meaning of an action is derived from the perceiver's perceptions of the actor's intention . . . which means that intentional harms, unlike accidental harms, are *meant* to cause pain.").

38. *See* PAUL GRICE, *Meaning, in* STUDIES IN THE WAY OF WORDS 213, 218–20 (1989).

39. *Id.* at 219, 220 (emphasis added).

40. Grice gives as an example: "If my college stopped my salary altogether, I should accuse them of ruining me; if they cut it by one pound, I might accuse them of insulting me." GRICE, *supra*, at 220. In the former case, it makes financial sense for the college to stop Grice's salary; it can save some money (perhaps it is financially strapped, perhaps it will eliminate the whole Philosophy faculty, etc.). Or perhaps the college really does want to "ruin" Prof. Grice. But whatever the motive (intention), it is presumably not primarily to "make a point," which is precisely what we would say of the latter case, which has no discernable basis in finances or other noncommunicative purposes.

41. BOY SCOUT HANDBOOK 160 (7th ed. 1965).

42. *Id.* at 161.

43. *Id.* at 162.

44. *Id.* at 161.

45. Tiersma, *supra*, at 1567; *cf.* Note, *Symbolic Conduct*, 68 COLUM. L. REV. 1091, 1117 (1968) (assertive conduct is often "a departure from the actor's normal activities and cannot adequately be explained unless a desire to communicate is presumed").

46. *See* SIMON BLACKBURN, SPREADING THE WORD: GROUNDINGS IN THE PHILOSOPHY OF LANGUAGE § 4.1 (1984).

47. KENNETH TAYLOR, TRUTH AND MEANING 315 (1998).

48. A number of philosophical puzzles will have to go unexplored here, but I will mention two: (1) My ideal of communication is a message that can be expressed within quotation marks. A nonverbal intentional action may, under certain circumstances, convey such a message. (See the preceding examples in the text.) This understanding of meaning is, I believe, the only one that can be reconciled with the constitutional case law. (*See* Parts III–V *infra*.) (2) Brison employs a

broader, "natural" sense of *meaning* that allows her to say things like "The twitching of the corpse meant that the person had recently died." It would be odd to put within quotation marks what the corpse's twitching meant. ("Help! I just died!") For another example, see Brison, *Speech and Other Acts*, *supra*, at 264 n.14:

> It seems any object or event could—in the right circumstances—be speech, including "found objects" and even natural events. (Shakespeare found "sermons in stones, books in babbling brooks.") A rainstorm by itself is not speech. But if I have told you that I will meet you at your house at 6:30 p.m. tomorrow if it is raining there then, the rain (there and then) is my way of telling you that I will meet you.

Here, the model of the speaker, speaking—so central to legal debates—seems not to apply. *See generally* GRICE, *supra*.

Grice's position has produced its critics, but generally they point to problems that arise at the level of formal, linguistic systems—which is where my analysis leaves off. *See, e.g.*, BLACKBURN, *supra*, § 4.2; JOHN R. SEARLE, SPEECH ACTS § 2.6 (1969); ROBERT M. MARTIN, THE MEANING OF LANGUAGE 85–93 (1987) (Grice accounts for *speaker's meaning* but not *sentence meaning*).

49. The sound of the siren is like an expression; its occurrence on any particular occasion is like an utterance (of the expression), whose meaning relates back to what the speaker meant in uttering it, which in turn relates back to the speaker's underlying intentions in uttering it. *See* Chapter 1, Part I *supra*.

50. STEPHEN SCHIFFER, REMNANTS OF MEANING 260, 251 (1987).

51. *Id.* at 250.

52. Indeed, Schiffer argues that the practice in question would have to be one that pertained to the language as a whole. *See id.* at 251 ("The paradigm of a whole-utterance-type is a sentence of a natural language, and most (so to say) of them have never been uttered; so when it comes to sentences, we cannot account for *x*'s meaning *p* in G in terms of what members of G do mean in uttering *x*."); *id.* at 260 ("[N]othing like [what was said about simple signals] can be said as regards a sentence, a *composite* whole-utterance-type that means *p* in G, for it may mean *p* in G even if it has never been uttered, or indeed never *could* be uttered (perhaps because it is too long or convoluted to be processed).").

53. Schiffer calls this "a neat self-perpetuating regularity," *id.* at 250.

54. *See* Chapter 1, Part I *supra.*

55. Michael S. Moore, *The Semantics of Judging*, 54 S. CAL. L. REV. 151, 253 (1981).

56. *Id.* & n.227.

57. *Id.*

58. *Id.*

59. *See* STEPHEN R. SCHIFFER, MEANING 119–36 (1972).

60. *Id.* at 119–20.

61. *Id.* at 120.

62. *Id.*

63. *Id.* at 130.

64. *Id.* at 123.

65. *See id.* at 132–33; PAUL GRICE, *Utterer's Meaning, Sentence-Meaning, and Word-Meaning, in* STUDIES IN THE WAY OF WORDS, *supra,* at 117, 124–29.

66. *See* P.F. Strawson, *Meaning and Truth, in* THE PHILOSOPHY OF LANGUAGE 110, 115–20 (A.P. Martinich ed., 4th ed. 2001).

67. GRICE, *Meaning, in* STUDIES IN THE WAY OF WORDS, *supra,* at 219–20. Likewise, in the other example mentioned above, presenting a severed head does not, in and of itself, *mean* something like "This person is dead," though anyone could certainly infer as much. *See id.* at 218.

68. Strawson, *supra,* at 112.

It may be that an intention-based theory cannot be extended beyond simple signals (noncomposite whole-utterance-types) whose meanings are not determined by the meanings of their constituent parts. *See* SCHIFFER, REMNANTS OF MEANING, *supra,* at 251, 260. But these limitations should not deter a legal analysis that takes symbolic speech as its paradigm case and focuses on the constitutional significance of speakers' use of language. The legal problem, after all, is to account for speech, not to derive a comprehensive theory of meaning or language.

To understand symbolic speech in the legal sense, it may not be necessary to know what speech act the speaker is performing or what propositional content the speech act has. *See* STEPHEN SCHIFFER,

THE THINGS WE MEAN 112, 115 (2003). It is typically doubtful that the "speaker" of symbolic speech has thought things out that specifically and tried to convey a message of that particularity (or one that would or could be so understood). In *Texas v. Johnson* (the flag-burning case), for example, the dissenters could deny that any particularized message was conveyed by the burning of an American flag. *See* Part V *infra.*

Nevertheless, dissenters are just that—dissenters—and flag burning is unquestionably speech for constitutional purposes. A legal theory of speech based on the limiting case of symbolic speech thus does all it is supposed to do: it provides a minimal but general definition of speech.

69. 468 U.S. 288 (1984).
70. *Id.* at 294.
71. Spence v. Washington, 418 U.S. 405 (1974).
72. *Clark*, 468 U.S. at 305–06 (Marshall, J., dissenting).
73. *Id.* at 296.
74. *Id.* at 312 (Marshall, J., dissenting).
75. Street v. New York, 394 U.S. 576, 616 (1969) (Fortas, J., dissenting).
76. *Id.*
77. Virginia v. Black, 538 U.S. 343, 352, 353–54, 357 (2003); *see* Part I *supra.*
78. 415 U.S. 566 (1974).
79. 418 U.S. 405 (1974).
80. *Id.* at 410.
81. 491 U.S. 397 (1989).
82. *Id.* at 405.
83. H.R. 2978, 101st Cong., 1st Sess. (1989).
84. *Id.*
85. 36 U.S.C. § 176(k); *see generally id.* at §§ 173–77.
86. I thank Al Martinich for prompting me to rethink this issue.
87. *See generally* Vincent Blasi, *Six Conservatives in Search of the First Amendment: The Revealing Case of Nude Dancing*, 33 WM. & MARY L. REV. 611 (1992).
88. Barnes v. Glen Theatre, Inc., 501 U.S. 560, 566 (1991) (plurality opinion).

89. Miller v. Civil City of South Bend, 904 F.2d 1081, 1089 (7th Cir. 1990) (Posner, J., concurring).

90. *Barnes*, 501 U.S. at 563; *cf. Miller*, 904 F.2d at 1090–91 (Posner, J., concurring):

> The record contains a videotape of the dances that the proprietor of the "Kitty Kat Lounge" would like to exhibit. The name of the establishment does not promise high culture, nor the fact that it is a bar rather than a theater, nor (a related point) that the compensation of the dancers depends on the number of drinks they induce appreciative customers to buy after the dance. The dancers are presentable although not striking young women. They dance on a stage, with vigor but without accomplishment, to the sound of a jukebox, and while dancing they remove articles of clothing (beginning, for example, with a glove) until nothing is left.

91. *Miller*, 904 F.2d at 1091 (Posner, J., concurring).

92. "Expressive" suggests or implies (in some contexts at least) an involuntary, natural manifestation. Consider the difference between crying out involuntarily from sudden, sharp pain and saying "Ow!" or "Ouch!" or any of a long list of curse words suitable for the occasion. Although the difference is perhaps slight, in the latter cases there is an element of conventional, stylized meaning and thus an implied context of communication. *See* Chapter 3, Part II *supra.* This form of communication, as Grice puts it, is "rather . . . more loosely connected with the state of affairs . . . suggestive, in some recognizable way, of the state of affairs without being a natural response of [the speaker] to that state of affairs." GRICE, *Meaning Revisited, in* STUDIES IN THE WAY OF WORDS, *supra*, at 283, 295.

93. *See* Part II *supra.*

94. *See* Part IV *supra.*

95. *See* Part II *supra.*

96. *See* Part I *supra.*

97. *See* Part II *supra.*

98. With apologies to MARSHALL MCLUHAN, UNDERSTANDING MEDIA: THE EXTENSIONS OF MAN 7 (1964).

99. *Miller*, 904 F.2d at 1099 (Posner, J., concurring).

100. JOHN CAGE, *The Future of Music: Credo, in* SILENCE 3 (1966) (1937).

101. *Miller*, 904 F.2d at 1092 (Posner, J., concurring).
102. 904 F.2d at 1089 & n.1 (Cudahy, J., concurring).
103. *Id.* at 1093 (Posner, J., concurring).
104. *See* Part I *supra.*
105. *See* Part IV *supra.*
106. *See* Part II *supra.*
107. *See* Dallas v. Stanglin, 490 U.S. 19 (1989).
108. *See* People v. Hollman, 500 N.E.2d (1986); South Florida Free Beaches, Inc. v. Miami, 734 F.2d 608 (11th Cir. 1984).
109. *Miller*, 904 F.2d at 1098–99 (Posner, J., concurring).
110. R. George Wright, *A Rationale from J.S. Mill for the Free Speech Clause*, 1985 S. Ct. Rev. 149, 168.

Chapter 6: Descriptions

1. *See* Chapter 5, Part I *supra;* Susan J. Brison, *Speech and Other Acts*, 10 Legal Theory 261, 263–64 (2004).
2. Robert Post, *Recuperating First Amendment Doctrine*, 47 Stan. L. Rev. 1249, 1252 (1995).
3. *See* Chapter 4, Part IV *supra.*
4. Spence v. Washington, 418 U.S. 405, 409 (1974) (emphasis added).
5. *Id.* at 410.
6. As noted in Chapter 4, Part IV, the subject of coverage has yet to be fully or adequately theorized. This book considers problems of constitutional coverage that arise in the context of symbolic speech. The minimal but general theory of speech developed in Chapter 5 may be regarded as providing necessary and sufficient conditions for constitutional coverage—in the context of symbolic speech, where the key question is "Is it speech?" But the further task of articulating sufficient conditions in other contexts (where coverage may be denied even when speech is concededly at issue) has not been systematically taken up by the Court. *See* Frederick Schauer, *The Boundaries of the First Amendment: A Preliminary Exploration of Constitutional Salience*, 117 Harv. L. Rev. 1765, 1800–02 (2004) (building on work of Greenawalt in criminal law); Post, *supra*, at 1252–55 (arguing that social context and medium determine coverage).

7. *Spence*, 418 U.S. at 411.
8. United States v. O'Brien, 391 U.S. 367, 376 (1968) (emphasis added).
9. JOHN HART ELY, DEMOCRACY AND DISTRUST 111 (1980).
10. 336 U.S. 77 (1949).
11. *Id.* at 79.
12. *Id.* at 78.
13. *Id.* at 79.
14. *Id.*
15. ELY, *supra*, at 113.
16. *Id.* at 113 n.* *Cf.* John Hart Ely, *Flag Desecration: A Case Study in the Roles of Categorization and Balancing in First Amendment Analysis*, 88 HARV. L. REV. 1482, 1497 (1975):

> The critical question would therefore seem to be whether the harm that the state is seeking to avert is one that grows out of the fact that the defendant is communicating, and more particularly out of the way people can be expected to react to his message, or rather would arise even if the defendant's conduct had no communicative significance whatever.

17. *Cf.* EZRA POUND, A B C OF READING 36 (New Directions ed. 1960) (1934) ("Great literature is simply language charged with meaning to the utmost possible degree.").
18. *Kovacs*, 336 U.S. at 81.
19. *Id.* at 83, 87.
20. *Id.* at 87.
21. *Id.* at 89.
22. *Id.* at 102 (Black, J., dissenting).
23. KATHLEEN M. SULLIVAN & GERALD GUNTHER, CONSTITUTIONAL LAW 1234 (15th ed. 2004).
24. *Kovacs*, 336 U.S. at 97 (Frankfurter, J., concurring).
25. 391 U.S. 367 (1968).
26. *Id.* at 369.
27. *Id.* at 370.
28. *See* U.S. Const. art. I, § 8.
29. *O'Brien*, 391 U.S. at 377, 381.

30. *Id.* at 376.

31. Ely, *Flag Desecration, supra*, at 1495:

> It involves no conduct that is not at the same time communication, and no communication that does not result from conduct. Attempts to determine which element "predominates" will therefore inevitably degenerate into question-begging judgments about whether the activity should be protected.

32. It is as if the same phenomenon were being viewed from the different standpoints of physics, chemistry, and biology. *Cf.* ERNST CASSIRER, 1 THE PHILOSOPHY OF SYMBOLIC FORMS 76 (Ralph Manheim trans., 1955) ("physical, chemical, biological knowledge *frame their questions* each from its own particular standpoint and, in accordance with this standpoint, subject the phenomena to a special interpretation and formation").

33. *O'Brien*, 391 U.S. at 376.

34. *See* Chapter 5, Parts I–II *supra.*

35. R.A.V. v. City of St. Paul, 505 U.S. 377, 390 (1992).

36. Clark v. Community for Creative Non-Violence, 468 U.S. 288, 298 (1984); *see also* City of Los Angeles v. Alameda Books, 535 U.S. 425, 454–60 (2002) (Souter, J., dissenting) (secondary effects).

37. *See generally* LARRY ALEXANDER, IS THERE A RIGHT OF FREEDOM OF EXPRESSION? (2005) (focusing on government regulations and acts taken for the purpose of preventing messages from being received).

38. *See* Part III *supra.*

39. *O'Brien*, 391 U.S. at 377.

40. *Id.* at 375.

41. *Id.* (emphasis added).

42. *Id.* at 381–82.

43. *Cf. id.* at 375 ("there is nothing necessarily expressive about . . . the knowing destruction of certificates issued by the Selective Service System").

44. 283 U.S. 359 (1931).

45. *Id.* at 361.

46. 393 U.S. 503 (1969).

47. *Id.* at 505–06.

48. Ely, *Flag Desecration, supra*, at 1498 n.63; *see also id.* at 1491–92.

49. *See* A.P. MARTINICH & AVRUM STROLL, MUCH ADO ABOUT NONEXISTENCE: FICTION AND REFERENCE ch. 1 (2007); Note, *Lessons from Abroad: Mathematical, Poetic, and Literary Fictions in the Law*, 115 HARV. L. REV. 2228 (2002).

50. *See* Chapter 5, Part V *supra.*

51. Texas v. Johnson, 491 U.S. 397, 400 (1989).

52. *Id.* at 404 n.3.

53. 415 U.S. 566 (1974).

54. *Id.* at 568–69.

55. *Id.* at 570.

56. Community for Creative Non-Violence v. Watt, 703 F.2d 586, 622-23 (1983) (Scalia, J., dissenting).

57. THE RANDOM HOUSE DICTIONARY OF THE ENGLISH LANGUAGE 438 (2d unabridged ed. 1987).

58. *Goguen*, 415 U.S. at 588 (White, J., concurring in the judgment); *cf. id.* at 588, 590:

> In the case before us, as has been noted, the jury must have found that Goguen not only wore the flag on the seat of his pants but also that the act—and hence Goguen himself—was contemptuous of the flag. To convict on this basis is to convict not to protect the physical integrity or to protect against acts interfering with the proper use of the flag, but to punish for communicating ideas about the flag unacceptable to the controlling majority in the legislature. . . .
>
> . . . And if it be said that . . . Goguen communicated nothing at all by his conduct and did not intend to do so, there would then be no evidentiary basis whatsoever for convicting him of being "contemptuous" of the flag.

See also id. at 593 (Rehnquist, J., dissenting):

> Goguen was convicted of treating the flag contemptuously by the act of wearing it where he did, and I have difficulty seeing how Goguen could be found by a jury to have treated the flag contemptuously by his act and still not to have expressed any idea at all. There are, therefore, in my opinion, at least marginal elements of "symbolic speech" in Goguen's conduct as reflected by this record.

59. Another example in this last category would be Stromberg v. California, 283 U.S. 359 (1931), discussed above. The *O'Brien* Court analyzes *Stromberg* as a case

> where the alleged governmental interest in regulating conduct arises in some measure because the communication allegedly integral to the conduct is itself thought to be harmful. In *Stromberg v. California* . . . for example, this Court struck down a statutory phrase which punished people who expressed their "opposition to organized government" by displaying "any flag, badge, banner, or device." Since the statute there was aimed at suppressing communication it could not be sustained as a regulation of noncommunicative conduct.

391 U.S. at 382.

60. *O'Brien*, 391 U.S. at 385–86.

61. Not all "speech" in the senses used in ordinary language is considered speech for constitutional purposes; and even that which is may sometimes be "abridged." *See* Chapter 4, Part IV *supra;* Frederick Schauer, *The Boundaries of the First Amendment,* 117 HARV. L. REV. 1765, 1769–73 (2004) (distinguishing the First Amendment's "scope" or "coverage" from its "protection"); FREDERICK SCHAUER, FREE SPEECH: A PHILOSOPHICAL ENQUIRY 89–92 (1982).

62. Spence v. Washington, 418 U.S. 405, 411 (1974).

63. *Id.* at 414 n.8; *cf.* ELY, DEMOCRACY AND DISTRUST, *supra*, at 113 n.*:

> What relevantly distinguishes the assassination and the window breaking from the others is not that they are not expressive, but rather that the harm they cause does not flow from the message the act conveys. An assassination or a window breaking is harmful even if no one sees an expressive element in it; an armband can lead to trouble only if people know what it means.

See generally United States v. O'Brien, 391 U.S. 367 (1968).

64. *See, e.g.*, Cohen v. California, 403 U.S. 15, 24 (1971) ("[W]e cannot overemphasize that, in our judgment, most situations where the State has a justifiable interest in regulating speech will fall within one or more of the various established exceptions . . . to the usual rule that governmental bodies may not prescribe the form or content of individual expression."); R.A.V. v. City of St. Paul, 505 U.S. 377, 382 (1992) ("Content-based regulations are presumptively invalid."); Police Dept. of Chicago v. Mosley, 408 U.S. 92, 95–96 (1972)

("[A]bove all else, the First Amendment means that government has no power to restrict expression because of its message, its ideas, its subject matter, or its content.").

Acknowledgments

1. Toward a Philosophy of History (Ph.D. dissertation, Yale University, 1978).
2. The main text was Victor Zuckerkandl, The Sense of Music (1971).
3. *See Origins and Development of Medieval European Epic: The Problem of Cultural Transmission and Transformation,* 9 Mediaevalia 45 (1983).
4. *See* John Chadwick, The Decipherment of Linear B (2d ed. 1992); John Chadwick, Documents in Mycenaean Greek (2d ed. 1973); *cf.* Michael D. Coe, Breaking the Maya Code (revised ed. 1999).

Index